A TALE OF TWO CITIES

A TALE OF TWO CITIES

The Dave McPherson Story

DAVE McPHERSON
WITH DEREK WATSON

MAINSTREAM
PUBLISHING

EDINBURGH AND LONDON

Photograph Acknowledgements
Pictures courtesy of *Scottish Daily Record,* Craig Halkett, Alan Peebles,
Giulio Saggen, Capital Press, *Rangers News,* Allsport

First published in Great Britain in 1996 by
MAINSTREAM PUBLISHING COMPANY (EDINBURGH) LTD
7 Albany Street
Edinburgh EH1 3UG

ISBN 1 85158 879 5

A catalogue record for this book is available from the British Library
Typeset in Garamond
Printed and bound in Great Britain by Butler and Tanner Ltd, Frome

CONTENTS

For Donna, Christopher and both our families

FOREWORD

John Robertson of Hearts and Scotland

Not too many players get the chance, or have the ability, to play for Rangers, and the greatest compliment I can pay Davie is to say that he's managed to do it twice and picked up a barrowload of medals along the way.

A lot of people have criticised the Ibrox youth policy in recent years and in the past, but Davie is probably one of its most successful graduates, signing from school and battling his way up through the ranks – then competing against the superstars Rangers were signing after Graeme Souness's arrival. He graduated from their youth system to the first team because he's a quality player.

It was a great surprise to everyone at Tynecastle when Hearts managed to persuade him to join us in 1987. Dave's been a fabulous ambassador for Hearts, along with his defensive partner Craig Levein and he has been a permanent fixture under a string of Tynecastle managers.

When the three-foreigner rule for European competition was brought in and Rangers were looking for the best Scottish talent, Davie's proven ability saw him back at Ibrox for £1.2 million. He had another great season there and won three medals as part of Rangers' treble-winning side. So it was another shock when we got him back for a second time as part of the deal which took Alan McLaren in the opposite direction. Hearts spent £750,000 of the £2 million they got for Alan in what was a great deal for both players and the club. We lost a player of Alan's ability, but got Dave back and it speaks volumes for the Hearts management at the time that they wanted Dave McPherson as part of that deal because they had to replace quality with quality.

I know he's got a deep feeling for Hearts and the supporters love him and see him as an integral part of the future so hopefully he'll be here for a few more years to come. Davie's been a good friend and a great team-mate and I hope we're both wearing the maroon jersey together for as many seasons as possible.

We'd already met before he arrived at Tynecastle, as we were both involved in the international scene at youth level. He was six feet tall even then and I was standing looking up at him from a slightly lower level.

I played for the Under-15 Scottish Schools side, with guys like Paul McStay and John Sludden in the ranks, against the slightly older professional youth team which included Davie, Gordon Marshall, Dave Bowman, Kenny Black, Gary Mackay and Eric Black. All the lads got on really well and that summer Dave Bowman, who I went to school with, Kenny, Dave, Gordon and I, who were all with Rangers at the time, and Gary Mackay went on holiday together. They should have called it Mad-aluf – we had an unforgettable time.

The big man was a poser even then. He had the best of gear and of course the open shirt to show off the hairy chest. Unfortunately his image took a bit of a battering when Gary tripped and poured a large dark rum over his white trousers. I don't think the stain's come out to this day!

We've been friendly as team-mates and opponents and now we've ended up as room-mates. I feel more like his butler at times, or valet, with the amount of clothes he has.

We've had some great jousts over the years; over the piece we've probably come out about even.

Dave's got more medals than me of course, but that applies to just about everyone at Tynecastle where we'd all love just one. In league games, the honours have been shared. I've scored a few goals against him, but he goes on about how I'm a dirty wee player and how he'll never forget the time I scythed him down in a tackle, ran away with the ball and then managed to claim a penalty. He just stood there laughing saying 'only you could get away with that'. We've kicked each other a few times, but that's only in the heat of the match because we're both desperate to win.

Davie's an awkward opponent to play against – he's six feet four for a start! I used to complain to referees about his elbows, but I was told that because of his height they just happened to be the same level as my head anyway. I can remember one match when I was waiting on a corner kick coming in and someone behind me kept tugging my jersey. I responded with a sharp elbow or two in the ribs and eventually I realised it was Davie.

'Wee man, where are we going for a pint after the game?' he asked.

Even then, there was a bit of kidology going on as I'm sure one of the reasons he was chatting away was to try to break my concentration.

But he's been a brilliant ambassador and captain for us over the years. He's shouldered that responsibility with Craig Levein. Whenever one was injured the other would step in. They're both big imposing characters on and off the pitch and I'm convinced Davie's got the qualifications to be successful in management because of the way he handles himself. He's got a deep knowledge of the game and I think directors and chairmen will be looking at him and thinking that with his experience and attitude, he would make a great manager. He's similar to Jim Jefferies and Walter Smith in that he's got a certain aloofness which would allow him to do that kind of job.

Like most defenders, Dave's job isn't the most glamorous position on the park and fans are slow to praise and quick to criticise, but he's a players' player and always has been. One of the funniest things I've seen was in Dave's first Edinburgh derby when he rejoined us. The Hibs fans were hee-hawing and braying away, insinuating that the big man wasn't exactly a thoroughbred and they were still at it when he went up the park and scored. Every single Hearts fan in the ground stood up and did the same to the Hibbies. Davie couldn't believe it as he walked back to our end – he thought our fans were giving him stick as well and didn't realise at first that they were being sarcastic!

I get that kind of thing a lot as well and I take it as a mark of respect. To me, if opposition fans want to bait you and hurl abuse in your direction a) they're scared you'll do a job against them or b) they've got respect for you, they know you'll do the business and they're trying to put you off. I reckon that's as close as you get to a backhanded compliment in football. Davie's big enough to know that and he can handle it. He normally gets his revenge anyway. And the most important thing is that he's very highly regarded by the Hearts fans.

When he returned to Rangers at the start of that fantastic run in the Champions' League and treble-winning season, he was playing out of position on the right side of defence. I can remember asking Andy Goram, who's a mutual pal, how he was getting on as rumours that he was coming back to join us started to fly. 'The Goalie', as he's known to all, was straight to the point.

'He's probably our best player right now. He's playing wide on the right and he's been absolutely magnificent even though he doesn't want to play there,' he told me.

Ironically, he was playing the best football of his career when Rangers sold him back to us for the second time. It appeased the Hearts fans when Alan left because they knew they were getting a quality player plus cash in return.

Even though centre-half is his favourite position, it's great for the side that he can play a variety of positions including right midfield. He's also been a relatively prolific goalscorer. You would expect the majority of his goals to be headers as he carries a genuine threat at set-pieces, but he's blasted in a few great shots down the years too. He's also set up more than a few goals for me due to the problems he causes opposition defences and goalkeepers and I have to say that for a defender he's been not a bad striking partner.

He's got Hearts and Rangers to the Scottish Cup final with vital goals along the way, last season for us in the quarter-finals against St Johnstone and of course against us in the semi-final at Parkhead to put Rangers into the treble-winning final against Aberdeen.

I remember the latter all too clearly. His header was stopped on the line then came straight back out to him. Nobody could believe it when he scored with his left foot – or that it was his first goal of the season.

What made it even more galling on that occasion was that we were winning comfortably with 20 minutes to go and Ally McCoist hit a wild shot over the bar which for some inexplicable reason the referee decided was a corner.

As Davie and I ran up the park together I told him 'how jammy was that. This is the kind of thing your lot will score from.' Unfortunately I was right and even worse, it was Davie who grabbed the crucial goal to send us spinning to yet another semi-final defeat.

Guys like him and Craig Levein don't get appreciated because they make their job look so easy. Davie's attitude is always 'keep it simple'. In certain situations Dave will knock the ball out of play and the fans will think, 'What did he do that for?' But his reasoning is that if the ball's out of play the opposition can't score and you can get the rest of the team back and get organised. At times he should get a bit more credit. He rarely makes mistakes and if he's having a good game he doesn't get any plaudits for it. His own standards mean that it's simply expected that he's going to perform well.

In my case, I can have a great game against Hibs and not score, but because I've found the net so often in the past people think that I've played badly because I didn't get on the scoresheet. Davie's the same because of the high level of performance which he's displayed so consistently with Hearts and Rangers. He has bad games, we all do, but because he's normally so solid it's highlighted.

He's definitely a player for the big occasion, be it cup-ties, crucial league matches or a derby game. Hibs–Hearts matches are even more closely fought than Old Firm games in Glasgow. There are times we've been under siege at Tynecastle or Easter Road and Davie's held it together and literally been head and shoulders above everyone else on the park.

His size means he's very imposing and even though he doesnae look quick I can assure you he is. He's a legend for his cavalry charges up the park. When he sets off on one of those mazy runs the whole crowd sits up. The amount of goals he's set up that way has been incredible and one of the most famous examples was his 90-yard run against Rangers in the Cup to set up a goal for Kevin Thomas.

He's a player for big games against the likes of Celtic, Rangers and of course the big European nights which we've had plenty of at Tynecastle in recent years. I can remember a fine performance against Dnepr when he scored one of the goals and I got the other in the home leg, also during that terrific run we had up to the defeat against Bayern Munich in the Olympic Stadium; and of course against Red Star this season.

In the following pages he might also mention a belter of a free-kick against Aberdeen, unless he's forgotten about it, another header against Rangers and some of the goals he's scored against Hibs plus another memorable one against Celtic at Tynecastle. Another story he never tires of telling is of his four goals for Rangers against Valletta on his European debut. But we're not having any of that, I mean how many of those Maltesers have won the European Cup – or are likely to?

Off the park, he's very much a social animal and likes a few pints with the boys. Sometimes you feel sorry for him because at six feet four you can't hide him in a corner and people always make a beeline for him. Even if you sit him down and stick a lampshade over him he's still noticeable and he gets a lot of attention from fans.

But he's always got time to speak to people and, like the rest of us, he takes time out for charities and schools. Recently he's taken up golf and I have to say that this is one area where he does need to work hard. It's going to take him a few years to win back all the money he's lost against Andy Goram, me and other lads.

But he's a big, friendly guy and his only fault is that he's a bit slow getting to the bar at times. He would also win his place in the side just for having some of the dodgiest haircuts ever. He's gone from the long Afro to the short Afro and back and I think he'd admit that the Mexican bandit moustache he used to sport was a huge mistake, but then again it probably went well with his hairy chest and medallion man image.

Tynecastle has more of a family atmosphere and even though he loved it at Rangers, I think there's maybe a wee bit less pressure on him. He took a bit of stick from some of the Rangers fans because he came through the ranks there and they didn't pay a fortune for him the way they did for other players.

The second time round when they bought him back for £1.2 million there was a bit more pressure on him, but he's got no worries about having a high price tag and why should he? He's proved his worth with his performances on the pitch.

His ambition, like the rest of us is to win a medal with Hearts. The way he's been treated by the club and the fans means he'd love to repay that with a trophy. We'd all love to take a trip through Edinburgh on an open-topped bus, with a bit of silverware to show off. Mind you, he'd have to duck under some of the low bridges in Gorgie Road.

Dave's now at the stage that if he's not at Hearts the season after next when his contract runs out, he'll cause some interest as a player-manager. And being his loyal batman, he might just have to take me with him!

To be serious for a minute, I'd like to sign off by wishing the big man all the best with this book, and say that I hope he gives a few of my classic strikes a mention, though they probably deserve a chapter to themselves.

JOHN ROBERTSON

1

HAMPDEN HEROES

Two of the proudest moments I've had in football came on 18 May 1996 at Hampden Park. The first was when the teams lined up in front of the famous old main stand at Hampden, where so many great players have graced the turf in the past, wearing a Hearts jersey at long last. The second came at the end of a hard-fought but ultimately hugely disappointing final when I looked behind the goal towards a sea of maroon and white, which remained long after the final whistle in a defiant and Heart-lifting tribute.

Forget the result and the mauling we took from a Brian Laudrup-inspired Rangers side. It was still our first Scottish Cup final in a decade, after so many near misses and it was a huge thrill to savour the unique atmosphere of such an afternoon. It was also a fitting end to a memorable first season for Jim Jefferies and Billy Brown during which we were the only side to beat Rangers twice and finished a respectable third in the League.

Jims' return to Tynecastle the previous summer was a real case of the return of the prodigal. The new boss is a Jambo through and through and he'd followed from a distance the various tragedies that have underlined the club's role as eternal bridesmaids. He'd also suffered a similar disappointment himself 20 years before when Derek Johnstone put Rangers ahead before three o'clock had even arrived and Rangers won 3–1 on their way to the treble. This time Rangers, with Gordon Durie grabbing a hat-trick and Brian Laudrup also outstanding, were again unstoppable.

It was still Hearts' first Cup final in ten years since they lost 3–0 to Aberdeen, days after losing out on the league title, so just being there was a magnificent achievement. There was no way we were just going their to make up the numbers though. Having beaten Rangers twice already in the league campaign, we thought we had a genuine chance, even though we were always underdogs. Losing 5–1 was a blow, but for the younger players at the club it was a great experience once they got over the bitter taste of defeat.

The biggest setback, of course, was losing Gary Locke so early through injury and there was nobody more gutted than him. To be without your captain for such a long period, especially a player of Gary's quality, was something that Rangers could maybe have withstood, but we certainly couldn't. We knew we were really up against it from that moment.

We had to reshuffle the defence with yours truly moving to the right. Later in the game the manager replaced Pasquale Bruno, leaving the inexperienced Paul Ritchie to hold the fort in the middle. To me, taking off a defender for a forward was justified as we were losing the game at that point anyway.

Billy Brown didn't agree with me after the match when I said that it didn't matter if we had lost 5–1 or 2–1 and put up the shutters, killed the game and tried to keep the score down. In my Rangers days we lost 1–0 in extra-time against Aberdeen when Eric Black scored with a deflection and, to be honest, I felt more gutted after that game.

We were well beaten this time round and there were no excuses. I took over as captain when Gary went off and briefly I harboured thoughts of going up the steps to collect the Cup, but it wasn't to be. We didn't freeze on the day, but we didn't play particularly well either and Rangers did. End of story.

Gilles Rousset came in for his share of criticism for losing a soft second goal to what looked like a fairly speculative Brian Laudrup shot, but Gilles has been outstanding for us all season and if it hadn't been for him the final scoreline could have been higher.

The build-up to the match was great. We retired to our training camp at Durham near Newcastle on Monday, Tuesday and Wednesday, where the whole squad worked hard in the sweltering heat. There was a great atmosphere, not overconfidence, but we were all looking forward to the big day and having the chance to nail the label of being a club who bottled it in semi-finals. After past disasters, like the clashes with Airdrie the previous season when we were dumped after a replay and the season before that when we collapsed against Celtic, we had proved ourselves just by getting to the final.

Nipper Lawrence was sleeping for Scotland on the sunbed and the atmosphere was pretty relaxed. We enjoyed a few beers after training was finished, before heading to bed early and there was a good mixture of young lads and experienced pros. John Robertson, Gary Mackay, Alan Lawrence (with Airdrie) and I were the only ones to have played in a final at Hampden before and even though it was still a tremendous occasion for us, for the rest of the lads it was the biggest game of their career.

It's always a worry with younger players, whether they're going to handle the big occasion or not, but on the day we didn't freeze, although we had played better as a team.

During the build-up, the funniest things were the live radio interviews the squad gave. The night before the match I had agreed to do a phone-in from our HQ at Dalmahoy country club just outside Edinburgh. I thought it would take ten minutes but it was more like 40. Normally it wouldn't have been a problem, but as I was sitting in the hotel foyer at a tiny table while all the rest of the lads had their dinner, it got a bit ridiculous.

No sooner had the announcer told me 'we're live on air, and Jimmy from Linlithgow's on the line', than the receptionist told me as the next call came through that I would have to move as a big private function was about to start.

'It's all right,' I told her. 'I won't be in the way.'

'No, you don't understand. We're piping in the first course,' she told me.

As the questions continued the skirl of the pipes got louder until the guy was actually right next to me. I reckoned it was fast turning into a disaster, but the radio people were quite happy to have a bit of local colour. Only problem is, half their listeners probably think the same kind of thing happens in living-rooms across Edinburgh on a Friday night. I couldn't hear myself think, but I had a laugh about it later and the rest of the squad loved every moment.

In another interview Alan McManus, Paul Ritchie, Alan Johnston, Kevin Thomas and I along with the management team and the chairman, were in the studio as Chris Robinson tried to answer a couple of serious questions. Despite having water thrown at him and the lads trying every trick in the book to put him off he handled it really well.

Another guy asked Kevin how he was doing after his injury. Big mistake.

'Fine,' said Kevin. 'But it would be even better if the manager would talk to me. Jim and Billy haven't spoken to me since I lost my place in the side.'

By the look on the management's faces it wasn't going to take long for that to change.

The boss got the build-up and everything else right in the run-up to the game, but in one area I felt we let ourselves down – our pre-match comments in the press.

Having been at Ibrox and seen the notice board there filled with articles from various sides proclaiming just what they're going to do to Rangers, I know how well Walter Smith and Archie Knox use that kind of psychology to fire their players up. With a lot of young guys in our team, who are obviously confident in their own abilities they're not going to give teams the respect they're due or otherwise, which is a good thing. But some unguarded comments and the headlines that go with them, can make the other team far more determined than ever and it can work against you.

No one could have criticised our Italian import, Pasquale Bruno, for his efforts on the day, but even though he's been a great buy for us, some of his pre-match articles worked against us in my opinion.

Another mistake was when we were 1–0 up against Rangers earlier in the season. I couldn't believe that Pasquale was playing keepie-uppie (or the Italian equivalent) with the ball, really rubbing it in, as it always backfires on you. Sure enough, fast forward and Brian Laudrup, who could probably have kept the ball off the deck all day, is repaying the compliment at Hampden.

It was nice to be the only team to beat Rangers twice in the League with a great show from Alan Johnston at Ibrox in our 3–0 win there in January and another great display in a 2–0 victory at Tynecastle in April. But in a way I would much rather we had lost those games and it had been our turn for a result and a chance to show off in the Cup final. I felt we got our fingers burnt that day. After we had trooped up to collect our runners-up medals, there were a few tears in the dressing-room. Paul Ritchie and Alan Johnston in particular were feeling the pain of gut-wrenching disappointment.

It doesn't matter if it's your first cup final or your last, losing it always hurts, but losing out in the semi-final is even harder to take and young players like them should be proud to have been good enough to get there. I'm sure they'll have other chances. The final word went to Chris Robinson who came in and told us, 'Don't worry about it. You've had a great season in the League, you've qualified for the Cup Winners Cup and you've done me proud over the season.' He was bang on. You couldn't criticise lads who had put in plenty of effort despite not producing a good team performance on the day.

The season ahead is a huge one for Hearts and in particular for some of our young stars. Getting on in football is all about being consistent – year after year, season after season. A lot is expected of them and they've got to improve and prove themselves all over again. You can't keep being hailed as the next big thing. One day you wake up and find you're 30 and one of the great could-have-beens. Football is littered with players like that. Players who could have been up there with the best of them if they'd put more into training and not let their first top team game go to their heads; and players who could have made the first team if they'd only shown a bit more determination. But I don't think guys like Paul, Alan or Gary fall into that category and if they can reproduce the same type of form they'll hopefully end Hearts' trophy famine at last.

As I said earlier, the fans' reaction, even in defeat, was superb and meant a lot to us. On a fairly subdued team bus in the eastbound lane of the M8, a stream of motorbikes, coaches and cars passed us as thousands of the 17,000 who were in the capacity Hampden crowd headed home.

Only one guy, who stuck two fingers up as he passed, didn't have a smile and a wave for us. The heroes' welcome that awaited us in George Street and the surrounding area as we headed back for a post-match meal at the George Hotel, would have made any casual observer think we had won the Cup instead of the Gers.

Thousands turned up, hugging us and shedding a tear or two, and it's at times like that you really appreciate the fans.

It was a humbling experience. They had all enjoyed their day, and were just happy we had got there at last and pleased that, up to a point, we had put up a fight. I don't think Rangers' punters would have done the same for their side if they had lost by a similar scoreline, but I think we have more of an affinity with our fans. We have a different type of support entirely. Although Rangers and Celtic have a larger following, the Ibrox fans in particular are more used to success, whereas the Gorgie gang are more familiar with letdowns, of which no-one needs any reminding.

People sometimes think that the Edinburgh clubs are split down the same religious lines as the Old Firm but, although there is a religious element present, it's not as clear cut as that. It's more a family thing with generations supporting either team.

Unlike at Ibrox where you're under pressure to win every game, and by a barrowload of goals, at Tynecastle, as long as you put up a fight, provide some entertainment and are seen to be challenging, they'll enjoy a few highlights during the season.

But, of course, even though they were behind us every step of the way on that road to Hampden and stuck by us afterwards, there's nothing myself and the rest of the lads would like better than to repay that support with a trophy; hopefully that judgement day isn't too far off.

2

JEFF'S JAMBOS

After serving under four managers at Ibrox and four at Hearts I reckon I'm more qualified than most to state that Jim Jefferies is the right man to bring back success to Tynecastle. It was a real wrench for him to leave Brockville where he was a real local hero and it proves just how much the Hearts job meant to him to be able to turn his back on the fans and everything he'd worked for there.

Jim and Billy's first game in charge following Tommy McLean's departure, was a pre-season friendly against Derby County. Billy came into the dressing-room before the game and said, 'Relax. Enjoy the match and don't overdo it – we don't want any injuries.

'Jim will be watching you from the stand, but don't feel under any pressure.'

We duly followed his instructions to the letter – and were 3–0 down at half-time! To be fair to the lads, we had all felt pretty fit, full of confidence and keen to impress our new gaffer when we boarded the team coach in Edinburgh. But ten hours later after a nightmare traffic jam on the M1 we just had time for a light meal before lights out, and we were still waking up when Derby started to demolish us. English teams are usually just ahead of us in the pre-season stakes, so while they all looked like flying machines, we were sluggish by comparison.

It was a slightly less cocky dressing-room when Jim came in at half-time and in best *Dad's Army* tradition the message was simple: 'Don't Panic!' He told us not to worry about the first half and to put it behind us and set about makng a few tactical changes. Gary Locke had been playing right-back and we were a bit exposed there, so we shuffled things around a wee bit and found ourselves right back in the match. Before we knew it, we'd pulled back a goal and we went on to draw 3–3.

Jim looked a lot happier at the end of the 90 minutes and I think it was a great boost for the manager as well as us to have got such a good response from the players. Don't forget, it was a big gamble for Jim to move and there's no doubt being able to bring that kind of turnaround in our fortunes did a lot for his confidence. Both he and Billy were delighted with the result. It was also the kind of result that might not have happened latterly under Jim's predecessor Tommy McLean.

Matters came to a head in the close season with a string of stories about Tommy leaving and Jim taking over. Denials were followed by counter-denials and defiance from Tommy who knew the writing was on the wall. Finally the should-I-stay-or-go saga came to an end and Hearts got their man.

The last thing the players wanted was to start the new season with any uncertainty, so although Tommy's departure was met with mixed emotions, we were happy to have Jim and Billy on board. Then we realised that you have to prove to a new boss that you're good enough to be in his team and keep your fingers crossed that he likes you. It's literally a whole new ball game.

When he arrived, Tommy McLean wasn't given the warmest of welcomes from some fans because of the part he'd played in depriving Hearts of the league title in 1965. But of course, not being a Jambo isn't something that could ever be said about Jim. He's a former club captain and was a great servant to the club before being handed a free transfer by the previous board, days before Wallace Mercer took over.

It's a professional game and you do your best for whoever pays your wages, but it does show and it does make a difference. The fact that Billy Brown's a local lad from Musselburgh, has stayed in the area for a number of years, and knows what the club and its fans are all about definitely helps. Jim's originally from the village of Wallyford just outside Edinburgh, though he now stays in the middle of nowhere in the Borders. They've both got a lot of feeling for the club, which can be a hindrance at times as I found out when I was with Rangers but it helped them settle in quickly, a lot more easily than they might otherwise have done.

When they arrived at Tynecastle, there wasn't a lot of money to spend so the manager knew he would have to deal with more or less the same squad for the season. He was quite cute and did his best to keep everyone happy. That's more or less impossible to do as everyone wants to play, but Jim did his best, realising that he couldn't afford to change things around too quickly and spark a mass exodus.

I'd met both of them once or twice before and, of course, whenever we played Falkirk, and got on fine with them. Then again, he never tried to sign me!

Getting things sorted out after a long period of uncertainty was a big boost for the club at the start of the league campaign. I reckoned we had a strong enough squad to do well in the Premier Division and a good mix of experienced and younger players breaking through.

Our first big test under the new regime was in the Coca-Cola Cup against Dunfermline at Tynecastle. They had beaten us two or three nil in a pre-season friendly behind closed doors and while results at that stage of the season don't really matter too much, it undoubtedly gave the Pars a lift going into the tie.

Hearts v Dunfermline down the years is almost like a derby fixture against our Fife rivals. They have traditionally been very tight, very close games and we knew this one would be no different. So getting a victory was a big bonus. It was a very entertaining game and before I forget, I grabbed the winner – a rasping left-foot shot from the edge of the box which was definitely one of my better goals.

Of course, the most talked about victories of the season came against Rangers, who've found us a bit of a bogey team in recent seasons. We beat them home and away scoring five goals without reply. Performances like that saw our young stars like Alan Johnston firmly under the spotlight. Playing in front of a massive hostile crowd at Ibrox or Parkhead is something guys like him relish. If you have any shortage of confidence, without being cocky, there's no point in being involved in football, you simply won't make it. Younger players are getting involved in pressure-cooker situations and the sooner you learn to handle that and the big crowds that go with it, the better player you'll be.

That memorable afternoon at Ibrox in January was my first back from injury and I must admit I had some doubts that I was ready for it.

'I'm fit enough to play, but whether or not I'm match fit for a game as tough as this, I'll tell you later. I'll play, but it's your call.' I told Jim.

I didn't think he would have brought me in as I was struggling for match fitness after spending two months on the sidelines, but in the end I was delighted to be on the pitch that afternoon.

We spoke about the match and all agreed it was a big one for the club and then the manager told me he was putting me in the back four and moving Frankie into midfield. For the first 20 minutes we were under siege and under a lot of pressure. I was really struggling. But after that initial onslaught I caught my second wind and felt very comfortable. On the day we played brilliantly and worked very hard for each other.

Rangers had a couple of chances early on and if they had scored it would have been a different game. With the talent they have in their ranks the only way to beat them is to close them down quickly, defend well and hit on the break, things we did exceptionally well that day. It wasn't a classic match, especially if you were a Gers fan or a neutral, but in terms of playing away from home, particularly at Ibrox, it was textbook stuff and for the Hearts fans it was a day to savour.

Alan Johnston certainly lived up to his 'Magic' nickname. He wrote his name in the record books as the first player to score a hat-trick against Rangers since John Brown in November 1985 for Dundee, and it's been even longer since anyone managed to do it at Ibrox

Strangely enough what a lot of fans probably didn't realise that day was that, like Bomber, Alan is a big Rangers fan and, although he was delighted to grab those three goals, he would probably have preferred to have done it at Parkhead. He was actually a wee bit down in the mouth about it.

'My pals won't speak to me tonight,' he said, before he found out he could keep the match ball which put a smile back on his face.

It's great for him to have something like that on his CV and he certainly deserved it. They were three magic strikes. The build-up for the first was superb and the other two were of similar quality. Alan might not be the fastest player in the world, but he'll certainly beat you with sheer ability and skill.

Results like that helped us finish joint third in the table, which was a bit more fun than facing a relegation battle the way we had in the past. But because we lost out on goal difference to Aberdeen for a

UEFA Cup place, we had to settle for qualifying for the Cup Winners Cup thanks to our Scottish Cup performances. European competition will be another first for our young guns and even though they performed well last term, I just hope they can cope with the pressure that's going to be heaped on them this time round.

Jock Wallace always used to say that the secret of carving out a successful career in football is simple – consistency. Football is littered with one-hit wonders who've shot to the top and then vanished without a trace in a very short space of time. You might not be the next Pele, but if you consistently deliver a high level of performance and commitment, you've got a real future in the game.

Paul Ritchie was probably the player who achieved that out of all our new kids last year. It's maybe slightly easier for a defender to do that, but if he can maintain the standards he set, then he's got a great career ahead of him.

Last season was a good beginning, but it's 1996–97 that counts now and they've got to prove themselves again and again in the seasons that follow. Our youngsters attracted most of the attention and grabbed most of the headlines last time, but without wanting to take anything away from their achievements I think a lot of people failed to give the more experienced members of the squad their due. It's okay trying to bring youngsters on, but I don't think they would have got as far as they did without the help of the more experienced pros. Obviously I'm included in the latter's ranks, but I'm not looking for any plaudits for myself. But everybody, I don't care what they do for a living or how gifted a player they are, needs someone to give them a wee lift and tell them 'well done' from time to time. That means more than anything.

There are probably more players at Hearts who could be described as 'great servants' than any other club. A few guys have been here for their entire careers; others, like Robbo and John Colquhoun, have been forced to leave, sold because of financial difficulties, but have come back to do a great job. Even though there are a few of us in the proverbial twilight of our careers, we've still got plenty to offer and hopefully are appreciated.

Although I enjoyed the season overall, I did have one run-in with our new gaffer following a 5–1 defeat against Partick Thistle.

Nobody on our side could have claimed to have played well, but the following week I found my name had mysteriously dropped off the team sheet. I asked the manager, but he denied I was being made a scapegoat. As I was the only change, it certainly felt that way.

I did get back into the side but at right-back instead of in the middle, so I wasn't overjoyed. I really don't enjoy playing there at all, and although you're supposed to be happy just to be playing, to be brutally honest I hate it at times. It wasn't too bad playing there with Rangers and winning the treble for your efforts, but at the stage I'm at in my career, I'd rather play where I feel most comfortable, not wider where you are more exposed. All the best games I've had for Hearts have been in central defence, including the two ties against Red Star at the start of this season.

When we lost 4–0 to Aberdeen, I don't think the defence was entirely to blame. We got a bit of reaction from our efforts in Europe and Aberdeen had two extra days' rest, as we played on the Thursday night. That was an important factor. In general we didn't look sharp and there wasn't much we could have done about the goals, two of which were deflections and, of course, a great free-kick.

Hopefully that will be a freak result. I think we have an even stronger squad for the league campaign this year. Despite the lack of cash, Jim's already made a few shrewd buys. No doubt there will be more on the way.

Gilles Rousset and Pasquale Bruno, have brought a more cosmopolitan flavour to the dressing-room.

Pasquale, or Frankie as he's nicknamed, and Gilles both came here looking for a chance to resurrect their careers.

Gilles had a few problems at Lyon, but since he signed on he's been outstanding and has become a real fans' favourite. He had a hard act to follow in Henry Smith who was a great servant to the club and played a record number of times in between the sticks.

It was the right time for both of them to come in. They took their chance and have done well, particularly Gilles. He had a great season and made a lot of great saves. It's just a pity that some people will remember his gaffe in the final long after they've forgotten how many vital stops he's made and how many games he's kept us in. He had a terrific start to this season with a fine display against Red Star in Belgrade. Off the park he's a very quiet big guy and although there was a bit of a language barrier at first, he's gradually overcome that and his English is improving. The good thing about him is he's keen to learn the lingo and he wants to stay with Hearts. He isn't desperate to head back home with a few quid in his pocket like some foreign players which is good for him and the club. He isn't the most vocal of keepers on the field but he's been a real bargain buy.

Following initial success, I think, like a lot of Scottish managers, Jim will be looking further afield than this country for fresh faces. After the Bosman ruling meant scrapping transfer fees in the majority of countries there will undoubtedly be a lot more foreign players over here, especially with the SFA still clinging desperately to the status quo.

Our players still aren't under freedom of contract and can't move freely between Scottish clubs which in my book is unfair and a restriction of trade. The new ruling the SFA have brought in which means even if you only play a trial game for a continental team you can't play in Scotland for a year, is a classic example of their misguided thinking. Instead of compensating in some way, it only makes matters worse and is actually driving our top talent away. Take Alan Johnston's case, for example. Having turned out for Strasbourg, even though they didn't sign him, there was still no way he could do a U-turn and patch things up with Hearts as he's not allowed back into Scottish football for 12 months. I hope matters will be resolved soon for the good of our game, our players and Hearts as well.

The day-to-day routine at Tynecastle has altered slightly over the years and under different managers. It can vary quite a bit depending on which training ground we're using out of the four or five available.

Eamonn Bannon discovered Pinkie Park in Musselburgh, which is a primary school with four or five football pitches, a rugby and a cricket pitch which is a great training area, but because it takes half an hour to get there and the same back, it makes a longer day.

We report to Tynecastle for 10.00 a.m. and, again like Ibrox, the best part is the crack you get in the dressing-room. First stop is the players' lounge where Robbo usually makes the mistake of asking if anyone wants a coffee, only to discover after a chorus of 'yes's' that we all do. His is usually getting cold by the time he's finished and then he has his first, but probably not last, moan of the day. Stevie Frail or I sometimes deputise for him and we're getting so good we're planning to open a coffee shop when we hang up our boots. On the other hand, some players, like 'Mickey' Cameron, would die of thirst if they had to make their own.

Craig Levein is a bit of a character and doesn't usually miss a chance to wind someone up, but after having a joke our main concerns are what to do if our lotto syndicate comes up trumps and who's hot and who's not in the golfing stakes.

I have to issue a warning here to anyone who might have to play Robbo at any stage that he's the club bandit. He claims to have a handicap of 8, but last year he played Carnoustie and shot better scores than a lot of the pros in the Scottish Open a few months ago. Nine over was the cut and John would definitely have made that.

At Ibrox, Graeme Souness was given credit for banning golf. Well that wasn't strictly true, but it was certainly discouraged. I could understand it as he wasn't keen to have players expending energy on a five or six mile hike when they had a game coming up. Even now I never play too close to a match and try to save my legs.

Like any club there's no shortage of laughs, especially at the expense of the younger lads. They're usually a bit overawed and nervous in the company of the more senior pros, at least to start with, but they soon learn to hold their own in the humour stakes. Two who'll remain nameless (they know who they are) were cornered one lunchtime and given a bit of a grilling. We hit them with a couple of general knowledge testers, among them we wanted to know who starred alongside Rhett Butler in *Gone With the Wind*.

'I ken who it is' said the first. 'Ronnie Kray'.

Before the laughter had died down his pal jumped in: 'Don't be so daft, of course it wasn't . . . it was Reggie,' he proudly announced to even more hilarity.

Another time one of them was asked what he weighed and he told us that it was 11 stone ten. All the time. He knew this because he weighed himself every morning and night. He was told that this was rare to be the same at both times of the day, that you were usually heavier or lighter, but he was insistent.

'In fact,' he said, 'I measure my height twice a day and it's exactly the same as well.'

We've got a lot of good youngsters at Hearts and some of them are going to be real stars, but to my mind there are too many these days who simply don't work hard enough. I can only use my own experiences as an example, but in the early days at Ibrox we were always back in the afternoon working on all areas of our game. You have to get the right habits at an early age or you won't last long. Sheer talent can help you break through to the first team, but to stay there you really have to graft. Clubs take in maybe 20 kids every season and if they're lucky, two will eventually make the grade. Out of the rest, some just won't have the talent, others will, but they won't make full use of it and will drift out of the game sooner rather than later.

There is a lot less respect for older players even though they've seen it all and done it the hard way. I don't want to come across as some autocratic elder statesman, but the only way to learn is to listen. I would never have dreamed of getting lippy with Tom Forsyth, Gregor Stevens or any of the senior pros at Ibrox and they would have been quick to slap me down if I had.

I believe the youngsters should have a lot more freedom to express themselves, but falling into the trap of thinking you know it all is a huge mistake.

Another bit of advice I'd give any young player is to take real care over any contract they sign. Okay, have your parents present, but get a good lawyer too. After 16 years as a professional footballer, I'm still having contract problems, simply because I haven't got some things in writing. I also think it's a better idea if clubs leave the manager to manage and let the chairman, who supposedly has the business experience, handle the contracts.

When I signed for Hearts the second time I dealt with Tommy McLean, but he had to okay everything with Chris Robinson, so I felt I would have been as well dealing direct with the chairman, as I had when I signed for Wallace Mercer.

Another part of our morning ritual is when John Colquhoun arrives and starts the latest rumour. He starts a new story every day, which is probably why he's moved into journalism as a sideline. There's absolutely no truth in any of them at all, but by the time we've finished training it's done the rounds and people are repeating his own gossip to him; All the 'you didn't get it from me, but have you heard the latest?' type stuff. As a result, porky pies are known in the Tynecastle dressing-room as J.C.s. His Sunday newspaper column is actually quite good, but we'd never tell him that. We prefer to slag him off for being the Hans Christian Andersen of football.

He does talk a lot of sense sometimes and he enjoyed a flirtation with the Labour Party a few years ago. A lot of Edinburgh Labour councillors including the Provost, Eric Milligan, are big Jambos and former Vice Chairman, Pilmar Smith, also had an affiliation.

So it's nice to see John, Labour man that he is, driving a brand new silver Mercedes. Some may call him a champagne socialist, but that's not for me to say.

Another useful addition to the squad has been Darren Beckford and I've enjoyed a few laughs with him in the short time he's been at the club. I've taken a few pelters for my haircuts, or lack of them, over the years and Darren insists that when he was younger his mum used to tell him that he wouldn't get an Afro like Dave McPherson unless he ate his greens. He also swears that he always tried to get me in his collection of Panini cards, just for my frizzy permed locks.

With fresh faces coming in, hopefully we can build on the success of last season and I think we have an even stronger squad, even though we've lost someone of Alan Johnston's ability. In the back four, I've already mentioned Gilles and Bruno and of course there's a promising youngster by the name of McPherson . . .

Another valuable member of the squad is Neil Pointon. We signed him from Oldham but he's also starred with Everton. Even though he's very experienced domestically, I didn't realise until afterwards that our tie with Red Star Belgrade was actually his first taste of Europe. Neil's got a great left peg and even though like myself, he's nearing the end of his career, he's still got a lot to offer. He's a really nice guy off the field and I've shared more than a couple of beers with him. He also spends a lot of time with the youngsters at the club and certainly has plenty to pass on.

Paul Ritchie, who celebrated his 21st birthday when we played the return match against Red Star at Tynecastle is a very talented youngster, although he's still got a lot to learn. He's got good pace, he's good in the air and is quite aggressive, but he still needs to work on his confidence on the ball which is something that will come with age and experience.

A recent signing, who I haven't seen too much of, is David Weir, whom Jim Jefferies signed from his old club, Falkirk. He's very comfortable on the ball and I'm sure if he works hard he'll also do well at Hearts.

Moving across the defence, Stevie Fulton is one of the most talented players I've played alongside, but he doesn't work just as hard as he needs to sometimes. He'd be the first to admit he does have a problem with his fitness and he doesn't do it often enough. But on his game he's a terrific player.

Steve Frail is another rising star. He's had a tough spell through injury, but he's come back and is starting to look sharp again. He's great going forward, a quality player.

Neil McCann is another recent signing from Dundee and again at the time of writing I haven't seen him play that often. But he's got great pace and is capable of delivering quality crosses and I'm sure he'll be a great asset in the season ahead. Like the Hearts supporters, I'm looking forward to seeing more of him.

Colin 'Mickey' Cameron is another Jefferies acquisition and I'm sure he's going to score a lot of goals for us. His best position is just behind the front two, but at the start of the season he played as a striker due to injuries. He gets in the box a lot for a midfielder and if he learns from my finishing he'll score a barrowload. It's also worth mentioning that the nickname comes from his ears which if you look closely resemble those of a certain cartoon character.

Up front of course, Robbo's still going strong although like myself he can't last forever, but when he's called on John will always be there to grab a goal or two.

And another veteran who's returned to the club is John Colquhoun. J.C. has been a great servant to Hearts and recently turned down a move to Airdrie to link up with Alex MacDonald again.

At present, I've taken over the captaincy from Gary Locke after his unfortunate cruciate ligament injury, but I've no doubt that Gary will be captain again when he's fit. Gary's a big Hearts fan. Jim's building his own team for the future and sees a bright future for Gary so he started by making him skipper.

Injuries have hit other players at the club among them Stevie Frail, Kevin Thomas and Craig Levein.

Throughout his career Craig's been unlucky with bad knee injuries hindering his prospects with Hearts and Scotland. It's good to have Kevin back with us and hopefully he'll be adding to his goals tally in the coming season. He's got great ability, but I think he needs more commitment.

He's fit enough at the moment, but he could be even fitter. In my opinion, he should be pushing himself even harder to make himself a better player. That's the reason he isn't in the first team on a regular basis. With a bit more effort he could be a great centre-forward, it's up to him.

Jim Jefferies is constantly trying to strenghten the squad and as I've said I think he's capable of bringing some silverware back to Tynecastle at long last. I get on fine with him, but like any manager who takes over, with the exception of the youngsters just breaking through to the first team, he wants to bring in his own men and build his own team – hopefully a successful one at that. He either fancies you or he doesn't and if it's the latter, there's not much you can do about it.

There was interest last season from Coventry, who wanted to tighten up their defence. But as I was injured at the time, it was a non-starter right away. I don't particulary think Hearts were desperate to get rid of me, but at the same time, Jim wants to build his own team and I think the cash would have come in handy. I've got a year left of my contract to run, so I'll have to wait and see what happens at that time and find out if I'm going to finish my career at Tynecastle.

When it comes to loyalty, players being loyal to a club, I'd put myself in that category, having never asked for a transfer or asked away from any club, but I've been sold three times! Fans have told me 'you left Hearts to join Rangers', but the truth of the matter is that I was sold and didn't get an offer to stay. I was made an offer to leave – it's as simple as that. I probably won't have the final say this time either.

It's been a long and winding, well pretty straight, road really: the south side of Glasgow to Edinburgh and then back from Gorgie to Govan.

But my first soccer journey was a lot shorter.

3

WIN OR BUSSED

These days, Ibrox players roll up to the car park at Ibrox a couple of hours before kick-off in Porsches and swish sponsored cars, via some leafy suburb or millionaires row. When I kicked off my career there it was the No 10 bus back to Cardonald, a few miles from the stadium in the south side of Glasgow.

'Haw, big man, dae I not know you from somewhere?' was the frequent enquiry as I headed home with my kitbag to my mum and dad's house.

They would have spotted the Rangers blazer and tie and probably assumed I was a steward until I mumbled, 'Aye, I was playing tonight.' More often than not they'd shake their heads and think I was spinning them a line, but it was true. If I had a penny for every time I've heard that, I'd have more cash than Chris Robinson.

But I didn't care. I'd fulfilled my boyhood dream and made it into the Gers first team. For a while though, it looked as if that just wasn't going to happen, no matter how hard I tried. When I was at school, though, I had no aspirations whatsoever to become a professional football player. Sure I enjoyed playing, show me a Glasgow kid who didn't, but having a good time, playing for the sake of it, was my number one priority.

I never took it seriously until I was 15, even though I knew I had a bit of a talent for it. But once I'd decided I wanted a career at Rangers, I worked hard at it.

As well as the school team, I was also playing with Pollok United alongside another member of the school side, Billy Davies. Billy had

33

already signed for Rangers, having been watched by a number of other clubs, including Manchester United, beforehand.

That was when fate took a hand. Laurie Cumming, the Ibrox chief scout who was a former Northern Ireland international, was checking on Billy to see how he was progressing. I must have caught his eye and before I knew it I was training with the Rangers youth side on Tuesday nights.

Laurie, who died shortly afterwards, did a great job for Rangers as did his successor, Archie Lawrie, in later years. I was sad to hear that Archie also died recently.

I've got a lot to thank Laurie for and after he gave me my break I never looked back.

It was great fun and even though most of the lads had their hearts set on a pro career, there were a lot who, through a combination of luck and being distracted by other pursuits, like wine, women and song, fell by the wayside.

Everyone was out to impress of course, especially when John Greig, who was boss at the time, made his monthly appearance at training nights. It was probably more of a morale booster for the kids, and perhaps a chance to see at first hand anyone who had caught Stan Anderson's eye, than in any actual coaching capacity.

But it was always nerve-racking to look up from the gym floor when you were doing your sit-ups and catch sight on the way up of a real Rangers legend.

Stan Anderson was one of the old school. He rarely had his hands out of his pockets and taught all the young hopefuls a lot at the Tuesday night S-Form training sessions.

When I became involved with the reserve team Joe Mason underlined just what was needed to make it at Ibrox. He'd make you run a lap of the track if you couldn't chip the ball into the goalie's arms. He pointed out quite correctly that if you couldn't chip the ball high enough and get it right on the training ground, there was no way you would ever do it for Rangers. There was no point in kidding you on, he'd say.

Davie Provan was responsible for the fine tuning with skill sessions where he developed your passing, control and touch. If it took all day, Davie would find the time until you got it right. He was a really nice guy and a great encouragement.

Unlike these days when the emphasis is on ball skills, the science that coaching has become was in its infancy; but neither were we treated the way that even first-team stars had been in the past when the manager refused to allow them to use a ball during the week with the upside-down logic that it would make them more hungry for the ball on a Saturday. We did some ball work, but in good Scottish tradition we did a lot of running in the pitch black in terrible winter weather. Looking back, it was probably character-building stuff, but we didn't think so at the time.

Again I must have done something right and the training certainly let the coaching staff find out how fast (or not) you were and how good your attitude was. Mine had changed by now. I'm not aggressive off the pitch, but I'm certainly competitive. When the time came to leave school I had the chance to continue my apprenticeship by signing on the ground staff full time, I had decided to give it a go. I was quietly determined that I could go further.

Even then there are a lot of doubters out there. Every time you pull on a jersey you're out to prove yourself, regardless of whether you feel you have anything to prove or not.

No matter how many Golden Boots and records Ally McCoist claims or vital goals he's scored for Rangers and Scotland, people still say 'Him? All he does is score goals . . . and he misses a lot of chances'.

The last Old Firm game I was at, I was sitting in the main stand at Ibrox and Charlie Miller's first pass went astray as did the second. And even though he's one of the most talented youngsters around, the two guys behind me were baying for blood 'For f***'s sake, get him aff.'

With that kind of outlook, you find out very early on that you have to give it your best shot every time you pull on a blue jersey.

Rangers farmed me out to Gartcosh United where I gained some valuable experience with a side who've turned out some terrific players over the years, including Derek Ferguson who arrived at Ibrox a few years later. Now that I was going into Ibrox with Billy every day and training full time I was a better and fitter player already.

There were a few other clubs showing interest but I had already signed for Rangers and I was delighted with that.

I'll never forget the first time I nervously climbed the famous marble staircase at Ibrox with my dad, Jim, and waited for the green light to flicker outside the manager's office at the top of the stairs. Red meant 'do not disturb' and we had a few minutes to drink in the unique atmosphere of the building and think about all the other famous names who'd climbed the same steps before being called in to see John Greig.

Sitting across the desk from him, underneath the stern-looking portraits of the previous Rangers bosses, legends like William Wilton, and his protégé Bill Struth, I nervously tried to concentrate on what John was saying. It wasn't exactly the words I'd been hoping for. He was quite blunt and said: 'I don't recommend that you sign for Rangers. I think you should go and get yourself an apprenticeship.'

To be perfectly honest, he didn't think I was going to make it as a player. A hatful of medals and Scotland caps later I think I can safely say that I proved him wrong, but then that was all in a future that few players are arrogant enough to dream about.

I told him simply that, while I was taking on board what he was saying, I wanted to have a go and that was it, I was a Ranger.

I was very stubborn and dedicated at that age and I ended up cutting myself off from a lot of friends, simply because I was taking everything so seriously. Girlfriends and enjoying yourself were the last things on my mind and looking back it was a very difficult time.

I wasn't the only player, who Greigy had doubts about. A few months later, I can remember playing in a trial match against Queen's Park with Richard Gough, who was straight off the plane from South Africa. John advised him that he didn't have a future at Ibrox, as he had plenty of cover in defence at that time, something I used to kid Goughie about years later – when he had become Rangers most successful captain ever, following good spells with Dundee United and Spurs.

I'm not knocking John. He knew that the odds are stacked very heavily against youngsters building a successful career, and on the strength of one performance he was unwilling to build someone's hopes up. You've got to respect him for his honesty.

In his defence, he did eventually sign Ally McCoist, who opted for instant first-team status at St Johnstone and then Sunderland, and he brought a few other valuable players to the club including Glasgow United's Ian Durrant who was later to make his debut under Jock.

The next step was playing with the reserves and here being taller than average helped speed up my progress. Like any second string it was a mixture of hopefuls and first-team regulars nearing the end of their careers, doing their best to claim any first-team chances that were going.

It was a tremendous thrill to be playing alongside famous names like Colin Jackson, Tom Forsyth, Tommy McLean, Alex Miller and Derek Johnstone to name but a few.

John Robertson tells a famous story about getting a bit lippy and cocky when he first broke into the Hearts top team. After making a fuss about one of the senior pros not giving him a decent pass he was a wee bit upset to find himself suspended by the throat in the tunnel and told in no uncertain terms that 'If I play the ball short, you come back for it and if I give it long, you f****** run for it. And never speak to any senior player like that again.' He got the message.

It was the same story at Ibrox and I was careful not to step out of line and to learn everything possible from the older guys around me. Coaches like Stan Anderson and Joe Mason commanded a great deal of respect and you would run yourself into the ground for them and Davie Provan. Their attitude was simple: work hard, train hard and listen hard and you would make it, otherwise, don't waste their time.

I had a lot of respect for them and my team-mates and at first I was maybe even a bit overawed.

I found myself playing the centre of defence alongside Tam Forsyth, who growled a few words of encouragement and told me to keep talking; we were to let each other know what was happening. Fair enough, I thought, and tried to settle myself. A few minutes into the game and the first attack came down my side of the park. 'Tam, here he comes,' I croaked, not sure whether it should be Tam, Tom or Mr Forsyth. As he charged across the box to snuff out the danger he imparted a few more words of advice: 'For f***s sake don't whisper . . . don't make it sound like an apology!' First lesson.

Guys like him, nearing the end of their playing careers, look over their shoulder at younger players like myself, but they were still very professional and gave you a lot of help.

And it wasn't just the experienced players at Ibrox either. My first reserve game against Celtic saw me lining up against Parkhead favourite Johnny Doyle, who sadly is no longer with us. Even though it was a second-string fixture, I was fired up for it and there was a fairly large crowd, both halves of which were baying for blood long before the kick-off.

Just before the whistle went, Johnny sidled up to me and demanded: 'Hey, big man. You know what this game's all about?'

'No,' I replied warily. 'Why don't you tell me?'

Without replying he pulled up his jersey and showed me a massive crucifix taped to his chest, at which point I burst out laughing. The fans probably wondered what the joke was, the two of us grinning away at each other when we were supposed to be deadly enemies.

'Don't worry. Mark me tight and you'll be fine,' he added. During the game he told me 'take it easy' after a couple of tackles and then at the end he shook hands and told me: 'Well done son. Thought you played well and if you stick in you'll do okay.'

Coming from such an unexpected source, it meant a lot to me. I thought it was brilliant, a really nice touch. I was getting ready to go into another rematch of the Battle of the Boyne and Johnny had defused the situation right away. I'm sure there was a clever bit of psychology involved in his antics at the start, but it was good crack all the same.

We went on to win the reserve league championship that season, which might not sound like a big deal, but to a youngster like me it was, especially in my first season. Coaches and managers always tell you that winning is a great habit to acquire at any level, but unfortunately the trophy cabinet never needed just as much spit and polish as it does these days.

The club was going through a fairly difficult time. Jock Wallace had departed under acrimonious circumstances after the club failed to recognise his achievements, among them two trebles, and John Greig, the man who had led the side on the park to those famous victories, was in the hotseat.

For someone as successful as he was as a player, trying to recreate that with a jacket and tie on was no mean feat. He had gone from being a friend and team-mate to gaffer almost too quickly. Other Old Firm players would go into management starting down the divisions and out of the limelight. But that was a luxury the club couldn't afford, and it made John Greig's job near impossible.

In hindsight, which is especially valuable in football, the club could have done with a clear-out and some fresh faces, but that wasn't really possible under the circumstances.

One poignant example was the rift that developed between John and Alex MacDonald who were great friends and team-mates.

Alex was a bit like John Brown in that he liked to be in as early as possible and take his time preparing for the match. One day, following his usual routine, he was in from the crack of dawn and was standing there already changed in the dressing-room when the team was announced and he wasn't in it.

Alex felt, rightly in my view, that he could have been told beforehand and been big enough to handle being dropped and deal with it. I think there was a bit of respect lost there because of the manager's naïvety.

On the other hand I had no such complaints. I made my debut under Greigy and I was loving every second of it, having gone from the youth side to the reserves and then training with the first-team squad in a fairly short space of time.

In those heady days I was on the princely sum of £40 a week, the same as my brother who was an apprentice electrician. When I made it to the first team my pay packet doubled and no matter what you do for a living, that's some pay rise! But when you consider the thousands a week that top stars are on these days, it was hardly a fortune.

I made the breakthrough on Wednesday, 3 September 1981 in the second leg of a League Cup quarter-final match against Brechin City. It followed a league defeat against Celtic as a result of which, Greigy wielded the axe. Out went Peter McCloy, Sandy Jardine, Gregor Stevens, Derek Johnstone and Willie Johnston. In came yours truly, aged 17, and a 19-year old, Gordon Dalziel. Just to let you know how long ago that was, here's the full team: Stewart, McClelland, Dawson, Forsyth, McPherson, Redford, Cooper, Russell, Dalziel, MacDonald, McLean. Subs: Davies, Mackay.

At the time, Greigy was quoted as saying: 'We must experiment. If I was relying on Saturday's team we'd never get anywhere. Rangers are 4–0 up, so this is a logical time to give youngsters a chance. I hope the fans will turn out to cheer the new lads.'

It was hardly the most convincing victory ever – 1–0 in front of just 3,000 at Ibrox – but I was described as 'impressive' in the match report afterwards which I was chuffed about. Less pleasing was the fact that we were booed off at half-time; eventually a 76th minute goal from John MacDonald gave us the win.

I didn't really care though. As a Rangers fan, to have played even one game for the club was my ambition and some 321 first-team appearances and 32 goals later, I can look back on that inauspicious start and smile.

I was actually quite laid back about making my debut as we were playing against opposition we were supposed to beat; although the one thing every player will tell you is that the pace of the game is much faster now, especially playing at the back where a second's indecision could cost you dear.

I went from playing in public parks to appearing in front of 40,000 at Ibrox in a matter of months, but it wasn't hard to keep my feet on the ground. Staying near Ibrox, I always caught the bus home and, as I've said, it was a weird experience when people spotted the club outfit and wanted to know who you were, then refused to believe this ridiculous story about playing that night. Never mind win or bust, it was always win, lose or draw and the bus for me.

When I went back to Ibrox in 1992 it was like a totally different club. The stadium itself was even more imposing and impressive. The famous brick façade now had a new top tier and the old ash indoor track had been replaced by a warren of coaching rooms, offices and first class treatment facilities.

First time round, you stowed your gear in big metal coat hangers and hung it up in the dryer. In those days you wore the same kit for a week. Now you get a fresh set for every training session thanks to Jimmy Bell and George Soutar and the girls in the laundry room. Simple things like that and the fact that lunch served by Tiny and the girls in the kitchen means the players spend more time together and are well fed on a post-Souness diet of pasta and mineral water have improved things beyond belief and made the whole set-up far more professional.

We went on to win the League Cup that year after beating St Mirren 4–3 on aggregate in the semi-final. Davie Cooper, with a free-kick and great lob from Ian Redford gave us a 2–1 win over Dundee United in the final at Hampden.

With guys like Alex Miller, Gregor Stevens, who was to receive a six-month ban in March after his latest red card, and Colin Jackson still at the club, I was never in contention for a place in the final and had to wait for my first medal.

I was involved in Cup action in February when I scored at Ibrox in the third round of the Scottish Cup against Albion Rovers with a 67th-minute penalty

The following season, I found myself back in the first-team frame and I made my league debut against Morton at Cappielow on 9 October 1982 in a 0–0 draw. Playing for Morton that day was Colin Jackson who had moved after nearly 20 years at Ibrox. On the other side of the country a youngster called John Robertson, aged 18, came on and grabbed a second-half goal for Hearts.

A few days before that I grabbed my second first-team goal with an 18-yard effort in a 6–0 rout of Kilmarnock at Ibrox. The 12–1 aggregate win set up a League Cup semi-final appearance against Hearts. We beat the Jam Tarts 2–0 in the first leg at Ibrox and 2–1 at Tynecastle where I came on as a sub for Bobby Russell.

The final was against Celtic in December at Hampden. I was keeping my fingers crossed that I would get a crack at my first medal, but I was gutted when Gordon Smith, who had been brought back from Brighton on loan, made the side and I failed to make the bench. A second-half strike from Jim Bett wasn't enough after goals from Charlie Nicholas and Murdo MacLeod and the only bright spot on a dismal day was when Greigy handed me a medal, which cheered me up a bit even if it wasn't the colour I wanted.

I did get another medal that season, this time in the Scottish Cup, but again it was silver and really as far as I was concerned, of no use to anyone.

I played in our 2–1 win over Forfar in the fourth round after we had beaten Falkirk 2–0 in the first step towards Hampden. And I stayed in the side against Queen's Park (2–1) and for the semi-final and replay against St Mirren. That rerun at Hampden was another nervy affair with Sandy Clark grabbing the winner in controversial circumstances in 118 minutes.

After the slap in the face of missing out on that League Cup final, Greigy couldn't leave me out for the Scottish Cup final against Aberdeen, but once again we found ourselves playing extra-time and another late goal featured.

I thoroughly enjoyed my first final and played well enough, but I was absolutely gutted when one of my great adversaries, Eric Black, scored the winner for the Dons in 116 minutes to give them the trophy for the second year on the trot. I was the only youngster in a team of veterans, which for the record was: McCloy, Dawson, McClelland, McPherson, Peterson, Bett, Cooper (Davies), McKinnon, Clark, Russell, MacDonald (Dalziel).

There were a few highs in reaching both those Cup finals, but in the League, things were at best, erratic. I went on to make 19 appearances in the first team, and while I enjoyed every second, I have to admit it was a real struggle.

These days at Ibrox, youngsters are drafted into a side packed with quality and are expected to (and nearly always do) win every game they play, but we faced some real problems. Eventually what was the biggest shock of my career at that time arrived when Greigy was forced out. I took it badly as he was the one who had given me my break, but the writing had definitely been on the wall and even as a young player I realised very early on that the price of failure was high. I found it hard to come to terms with as he had been such a father figure to me.

One particularly bad moment came on 17 September in the 1983–84 season after a home match at Ibrox, another lacklustre performance which saw us crash 2–0 to the Dons. It was a hot day and the dressing-room windows which face on to Edmiston Drive were open. To everyone's embarrassment all you could hear was a group of disgruntled supporters chanting 'Greigy, Greigy, get to f***' which was demoralising for all of us.

We were third bottom of the League with only one point from our opening four games and even though we bounced back to beat St Johnstone 6–3 the following week, the fact that there were only 12,500 in what, after redevelopment, had become a fine stadium, tells its own story. In contrast, Alex MacDonald had led Hearts to five wins out of six over at Tynecastle where he had switched his allegiances after 12 years with Rangers.

We thumped Valletta and then knocked champs Dundee United off the top of the table with a 2–0 win. But even scoring 18 goals in a week wasn't enough!

We went on to lose 3–2 at Dens Park against Dundee. Craig Paterson, who had joined us from Hibs, and I took a lot of flak for that one, before losing 2–1 against Motherwell, which sparked another demonstration.

This time there were about 1,000 fans involved and over 60 cops keeping an eye on them. It was a terrible day for everybody and most of the players escaped by a side entrance, although Ally and Coop braved the front door. Even the reserves, who had won at Fir Park had to run the gauntlet.

It simply underlined the fact that there was no way the fans were going to accept John as manager for the rest of the season. Big Jock, who had returned to Scotland as Motherwell manager had been greeted like the messiah and got a warmer welcome than John when they took to the dug-out, was the fans' choice.

He wasn't the board's though. They tried to lure both Jim McLean and Alex Ferguson before Jock finally got the call he had been waiting for all along. Jim's brother Tommy, our assistant manager, took over for a league game against St Mirren, where we were an even bigger shambles and lost 3-0, a European tie against Porto which we won 2–1 at Ibrox and a 2–1 defeat at the hands of Celtic at Ibrox.

Although I think he would have liked to have been in the frame for the job, it was obvious that the board were thinking along different lines. Tam wanted it, his brother had been offered it and eventually Jock took it.

The players all knew things weren't going well but it was still a huge shock when John called a very emotional team meeting in the dressing-room and told us he was resigning, presumably having been pushed towards doing the honourable thing by the directors.

John was the man who had brought me to the club and it was a horrendous experience to know that he would no longer be around. Winning two Scottish and League Cups apiece and achieving a highest league position of second in his first season weren't enough.

Because I was the youngest in the dressing-room I wasn't really close to the rest of the players so even though the world had just ended as far as I was concerned, I couldn't share my feelings with them, even though a few of them were in tears, too.

Instead I got hold of a bottle of whisky and got drunk with one of my pals, the first time I had ever really been drunk. I raised more than one glass to Greigy that night, and he deserved every toast, not just for everything he'd done for me personally, but also for the way he handled himself during the bad times. He never tried to shirk the blame and somehow kept his famous sense of humour.

Eventually I was left with a hangover to end all hangovers. And as I was soon to discover, the only other thing that could make me feel as ill as that, was a day spent with Big Jock in sunny Gullane.

4

BIG JOCK

Out of all the medals and caps I've won in my career, pride of place on my mantlepiece is reserved for a souvenir of my spell under Big Jock, who was a great character on and off the pitch.

Now the big man was one of the hardest guys I've ever met and a lot of people saw that side to him; but he was also fair and a very generous, honest and even emotional man.

People didn't see that other side very often, especially the emotional bit. I'll never forget when I was getting married at 21 the big man called me into his office. Now, I was never in there, I never had any reason to be, so I was a bit worried about the reasons for my invitation. But I needn't have bothered. Our exchange happened so fast there couldn't have been more than 30 seconds between the big gruff voice telling me to come in and the door closing behind me.

Without any small talk he brusquely handed me a brown paper parcel tied up with string – no frills of course.

'Here, take that.'

'What is it, Gaffer?'

'What does it look like? It's a bloody wedding present from me and Daphne,' he rapped, before adding 'Don't tell anyone I gave you it.'

I thanked him and went back down the stairs to the dressing-room shaking my head and chuckling to myself, thinking he was some man. He didn't want anyone thinking he'd gone soft, even though at heart, I think he always was capable of great generosity.

Out of all the memories and medals I have, that present, which turned out to be an ornament still has pride of place.

Of course it means even more now that the big man's gone. His death while this book was being written made me think back to a lot of happy days working under him. Apart from two famous trebles and all the other trophies he brought to Ibrox, Jock will always be remembered for his infamous training sessions on the sands of Gullane.

But in my time under the big man, we also saw our fair share of deserts and far-flung foreign battlefields. The song used go 'Sandy, Sandy . . . Sandy in Royal Blue', and I think Jock took that to heart!

When Greigy left and eventually Jock got the job, it was a nervous time for everybody. I got on very well with John and felt comfortable working under him, but Jock was going to be a different story. He had a reputation second to none and we'd heard all the stories.

To my great relief we hit it off right away. My career actually got better – I couldn't believe it. With John you'd get a bawling out and a fine if you stepped out of line, but with Jock you knew a swift right hook was also a distinct possibility. Fortunately, I didn't have to find out first hand.

Jock was the manager who showed me the world. I had never left Britain before I joined Rangers and my first trip abroad was a six-week tour to Australia. We also ended up causing our own desert storm on a trip to Iraq and Jordan.

First time round, Jock had left unceremoniously after bringing the second treble to Ibrox, and moved to Leicester City. The reasons for his departure were never made official, but obviously he had been made a better offer. If players weren't getting a signing-on fee at that time, clubs certainly weren't splashing out where the manager was concerned.

Jock was a shrewd man and to my mind he had a perfect right to go. If you equate the success he brought the club in his first spell as boss with the money even mediocre managers are earning now, he would undoubtedly be heading for millionaire status, but at that time there was nothing like the cash there is in the game these days.

Not that that would ever have meant anything to Jock anyway. He would probably have done the job for nothing. I think it was more a matter of pride and how much the board wanted to keep him, than the cash involved, that saw him turn his back on the club.

Jock was one of the toughest and most uncompromising men I've ever met. But by all accounts when he came back to the club he'd actually mellowed and judging by some of the stories, he was a lot harder first time round.

Of course the ultimate symbol of the Wallace creed was the sands of Gullane. All pre-season training is tough, but Murder Hill as it was dubbed by the players, was your worst nightmare. For Jock it was the cornerstone of his training programme and he even built a replica using a couple of tons of sand down at Leicester!

I was down at Gullane not so long ago and I have to admit it didn't look as steep as I had remembered, but then again when you saw it year after year you probably got used to it. When I first clapped eyes on it though, I couldn't believe it. What made it even worse was Jock's off-the-cuff style. None of this scientific approach to shuttle runs and times and recovery periods.

Instead he'd growl 'Right, I want you to get up there . . . back to here . . . up to there and then the same again.' Now that would just be the first group of four. By the time the second group were ready to go he had forgotten what he'd given you! It was all off the top of his head and you could end up doing either twice as much or half what the other lads had been given.

The plus side was that after a gruelling session he would treat you to lunch at a hotel in Gullane and buy you a pint. He was brilliant for that type of thing and in return all you had to do was give him your best shot.

Greigy was actually one of the more modern managers and was interested in building a footballing, European-style side and building from the back. Of course, he was hampered in this by the fact that he had a lot of players who were set in their ways – a lot of very successful players who'd been at Ibrox for years and been former team-mates. As a result he was in an impossible position when it came to bringing in fresh blood and ideas.

But Jock stuck by the methods that had served him so well in the past and he was more gung ho as you would expect from an old jungle fighter. 'Close them down, work hard and score goals,' was about as complicated as your pre-match instructions got. It was all unplanned and tactics never really came into it. Having said that, there's a lot to be said for concentrating on your own strengths and not worrying about the opposition and when it came to motivation, Jock was the ultimate.

Everyone who played under the big man has their own favourite story and memory of him. Personally I'll never forget his impromptu fitness tests. There you were minding your own business when you'd meet the Gaffer on the marble stairs. 'Right, fitness test, now!' he'd tell you before whacking you as hard as he could in the guts, which was pretty hard. If you flinched you weren't fit enough!

The only thing to do was smile through gritted teeth. Then once he'd disappeared into his office you'd walk round the corner and double up in agony.

Every day he would gather all the players, including the younger lads, in the home dressing-room and put you through 300 press-ups and sit-ups and all sorts of exercises just to warm you up. But even if you hated every second, it definitely got you fit. Alex MacDonald and even Jim Jefferies stick by similar routines. They're not happy unless you're running up hill and down dale, even though a lot of other managers have moved on to more modern methods, with timed sprints and a more scientific approach.

If John Greig had given me my start, it was Jock who brought me my first medal, playing me in midfield in the League Cup final against Celtic.

There was a tremendous build-up for the match and Jock never missed a chance to hype things up in the press or in the dressing-room. But then again, all he had to do to get you motivated was look at you. His more famous team-talks all had a familiar theme.

'I want you to go out there and get the bastard. Grab him by the head, stick him under the water and let him drown, bring him up, cut his throat, put him back under the water, pull him out and then stab him in the guts. Now go get them.'

'Right, where's my Gurka knife,' you'd think. Not too sure if you were fighting a war or playing a football match.

His time in the army had moulded Jock into what he was. I wouldn't have liked to meet him in a dark corner, but if you were in trouble you couldn't have a better ally.

However, with all his experience in coaching and management, second time round, fiery team-talks might have got the best out of the players, but on occasions over the next two and a half seasons that best simply wasn't good enough.

I don't think he had a strong enough squad at his disposal and even though he wanted to buy players, the cash wasn't made available to him. The board were probably still living in the past in that respect and the money he had to spend didn't get him world-class players, although he did make several shrewd signings. He did build good Cup teams, but in the Cup more than the League a little luck can go a long way and we weren't good enough for the Premier Division.

After a torrid time of it in Greigy's last days and the aftermath, Jock settled back into the hotseat and led us on his first mission – to Pittodrie, where we were duly gubbed 3–0 denying him a winning start to his second spell.

But ten days afer the Ibrox board had agreed compensation of £125,000 with Motherwell and a salary reputed to be around £60,000, Jock was back at his beloved Ibrox on 19 November 1983 for a 0–0 draw with Dundee United. To give you some idea of the personnel at that time, the team was: McCloy, Nicholl, McClelland, McAdam, Dawson, McPherson, Prytz, Russell, Redford, McCoist, Clark, Cooper.

In December, Bobby Williamson made his debut in a 3–0 win over Jock's old club, Motherwell, and followed it up with a 2–1 win over Dundee which gave us our fourth win on the trot for the first time in five years.

Jock also brought in big Nicky Walker, who had played for him at Leicester City, and the club was certainly looking to the future with more confidence than we had done previously.

Greigy had spent around £1.5 million during his spell as manager to build what had been described as the 'costliest side in the history of Scottish football'! These days that wouldn't get you a reserve player. Jock also had some money to spend, though not a fortune by anyone's standards and again the problem was that any real stars in the Scottish game were being lured south by the big bucks offered by English First Division sides. But he did manage to bring in Stuart Munro from Alloa, who turned out to be a great buy in the coming seasons, and at the end of the season, enticed Iain Ferguson and Cammy Fraser from Dundee, who were worth £200,000 and £165,000 a tribunal decided.

Behind the scenes there were changes too, with Tommy McLean, Joe Mason and Davie Provan out and Alex Totten and John Hagart taking over coaching duties.

After being on the losing side against Celtic in my Old Firm debut at the start of the season, when Coisty opened the scoring after 33 seconds, and again under Tommy McLean, I finally tasted league victory against our old rivals in April 1984. Bobby Williamson scored with a spectacular overhead kick and Jimmy Nicholl was sent off in his last game before he returned to Toronto Blizzard. Down to ten men John McClelland, Craig Paterson and I had a busy half hour, but did well enough to keep them out and snatch the win.

Just before that I finally got my first winner's medal when we beat Celtic in the final of the League Cup. We saw off Queen of the South, Clydebank, Hearts and St Mirren before beating Dundee United in a replay in the semis with Sandy Clark and Ian Redford grabbing the goals to give us a 3–1 win on aggregate.

The final itself was a classic and a young striker called McCoist, who was gradually endearing himself to the Ibrox support, grabbed a hat-trick in a 3–2 win. We were 2–0 up, but Reid and McClair sent the match into extra-time. And in a dramatic finish, with just four minutes left on the clock, Roy Aitken brought down Coisty in the box. My heart was in my mouth when Pat Bonner saved his spot kick, but like everyone else on the terraces I went wild when he followed up to bang in the vital winner.

The team was: McCloy, Nicholl, Dawson, McClelland, Paterson, McPherson, Russell, McCoist, Clark (McAdam), MacDonald (Burns), Cooper.

There was another dramatic clash with Celtic at the tail end of the following season when Cooper and Dawson were sent off. McInally scored for Celtic, but we had Big Roy and Ally to thank again when the Celt conceded another penalty after missing one with just two minutes gone; and Ally grabbed another goal in the 77th minute.

All in all it wasn't a bad end to the season after a traumatic start. I was quite happy with my own tally of 54 appearances in all competitions, and eight goals wasn't too bad in my first full season at the club.

Jock's first season in charge saw us finish fourth in the table behind Aberdeen, who had set a new Premier Division record of 47 points, Celtic and Dundee United.

We had improved, but still not enough.

The following season it was a similar story. We finished fourth in the League behind the same three clubs, recaptured the League Cup again, but made early exits in the Scottish Cup and Europe.

We started really well, losing only twice in our first 20 games, but the second half of the season was a shocker. We only won four more league games and struggled against the clubs at the top of the table.

A big shock was the departure of Irish international John McClelland for Watford, after a great display against Inter Milan, where a 3–1 win at Ibrox wasn't quite enough for the next round.

The big man had wanted a signing-on fee of £40,000 for signing a new four-year contract, something the board, led by Chairman Rae Simpson, were never going to agree to, even though Jock backed his claim.

John was a real character with a wealth of experience, including a stint for Northern Ireland in the 1982 World Cup finals, but he always had a keen eye for making the maximum return for his efforts. He was keen to stay at Rangers, but he was also desperate for a signing-on fee. When the board knocked him back, he actually had a T-shirt printed which said 'All I want is a signing-on fee', and on the back 'OR I WILL LEAVE'. He wore it on the bus on the way to away games. I thought it was a bit naughty, but he made his point. Unfortunately he never got his way and headed south instead.

He wasn't the only one to lose out. John Paton, who became the next chairman flew to Toronto to persuade me to sign a new five-year contract with the promise of a signing-on fee for putting pen to paper. Being a young boy I took him at his word, but of course I never saw a penny.

Around that time Robert Prytz used to complain that compared to some clubs Rangers didn't pay good money or signing-on fees.

'All you get is "play for the jersey", but I say to Jock "I will go to the building society on Monday and hand the manager a Rangers jersey and say 'This pays for my mortgage.'"'

He had a point.

There was plenty of off-the-field dissent, but on the park things weren't too clever either. The Skol Cup was the one chink of light for us. The campaign started well when I scored in a 1–0 win over Falkirk at Ibrox and we blasted our way past Raith Rovers (4–0) and Cowdenbeath (3–1) to face Meadowbank Thistle in the semi-finals.

The Edinburgh minnows put up a tremendous fight in the second leg after we won the first 4–0. They took the lead and we struggled with ten men before Coisty popped up with five minutes to go to equalise and give the scoreline some respectability.

The final was played on 28 September and I was well pleased to collect the man-of-the-match trophy as well as a winners' medal at the end of it.

Having already collected a winners' medal against Celtic, like the rest of the lads I was confident that if we could beat Celtic we were capable of beating United.

It was a soaking wet afternoon and the final was played in atrocious conditions, but Iain Ferguson scored the all-important winner in 44 minutes after good work from Bobby Russell and Ian Redford. Iain Ferguson beat Hamish McAlpine with an unstoppable drive to separate the teams and we clung on to that slender lead for the second half to win the Cup. That winning team was: McCloy, Dawson, McClelland, Fraser, Paterson, McPherson, Russell (Prytz), McCoist, Ferguson (Mitchell), Redford, Cooper.

That and the win against Celtic went a long way to making up for the disappointment of my first Cup final, when we lost to Aberdeen in the Scottish Cup under John Greig. Everyone was really gutted when we went back to Ibrox that day. I felt even worse as I was leaving the next day to join the Scotland youth squad for the world finals in Mexico. The only person who thought to wish me luck was Ibrox legend Willie Waddell, for which I'm eternally grateful.

At that time I could really have done with someone to put their arm round my shoulders and tell me not to worry, there would be other times; but everyone else was so gutted themselves I was on my own and I walked out the front door that night on a real downer.

The aftermatch celebrations when we won those trophies under Jock meant a plate of sandwiches, the Govan True Blues Flute band and a songsheet with everyone, even the players' wives doing a turn. That changed when Souness arrived. Then it was a lavish meal, free-flowing champagne into the wee small hours and Wet Wet Wet as the house band.

In the League and Scottish Cup though, there was little cause for celebration. Coisty was top scorer again with 12 league goals, but even though Derek Johnstone came back from Chelsea, finding the net was proving to be a huge problem for us.

In February we hit a new low as John Brown dumped us out of the

Cup with a ninth-minute goal in the fourth round and the abuse from the stands was back at the same levels as it had been before Jock's arrival.

As has been well documented, that had to be the worst afternoon of the season with the fans howling for Coisty's blood after a string of misses. Even though he bore the brunt of their frustration, I think the rest of us have to shoulder just as much blame for what was a terrible display.

The previous month hadn't been memorable either and one match I would rather forget is a trip to Pittodrie where we lost 5–1 to the Dons with Derek Johnstone making his comeback. I'm sure the big man wished he was 500 miles away at Stamford Bridge that day.

Jock had tried to change things around and bring in new blood. Sandy Clark and Gregor Stevens were on their way out, to Hearts and Motherwell, along with John McClelland and later Davie Mitchell, while Ted McMinn arrived from Queen of the South for £100,000. Young hopefuls like Ian Durrant and Derek Ferguson made their first-team breakthroughs.

But the old Wallace magic that had brought him previous successes had gone and the following season, which turned out to be his last was even more disappointing.

We finished fifth in the League, with the campaign all but over by Christmas, went out in the first round of Europe against Atletico Osasuna and failed to make the final of the Scottish or League Cup, losing out to Hibs in the semi-final of the latter. There was the consolation prize of two Glasgow Cups. Beating Queen's Park 5–0 at the start of the season, after the competition had been delayed, wasn't much to write home about. By the time we faced Celtic in the last game of the season and collected the trophy again thanks to a Coisty hat-trick, the big man had gone and instead Graeme Souness made his Old Firm managerial debut.

One of the few highlights of the league campaign was beating Celtic 3–0 in November at Ibrox thanks to goals from Durranty, Coop and Ted McMinn, with both Ian and Derek Ferguson in great form.

Of course we blew it, losing by the same scoreline to Hearts the following week when we faced a few familiar faces in the Hearts line-up. Ex-Gers Sandy Clark got some revenge for his transfer by grabbing a double, and Sandy Jardine played his 1,000th senior game.

The following week John Brown scored his famous hat-trick for Dundee at Ibrox as we crashed again, this time 3–2.

We lost to Celtic in the Ne'erday fixture before honours were shared in the famous 4–4 game on 22 March. That was one of the most exciting games I've ever been involved in, though I'd much rather we hadn't lost four goals!

Even then, I think Jock knew he was running out of time. His last league match was another defeat, 3–1 at Tynecastle before a shocker against Spurs in a friendly finally spelled the end.

David Holmes, who had taken over from John Paton as Chairman was the man entrusted with the task of bringing success back to Ibrox and, while I had great respect for both of them, I think he knew that he was going to be the man to end Jock's Rangers days; and he wasn't a fan. The story goes that after a frosty first meeting, in the aftermath of that 4–4 draw with Celtic, Jock had commented that it was great stuff and fantastic entertainment for the fans. Holmes agreed then pointed out that perhaps it would have been even more entertaining if we had held on to our 4–3 lead and won the game.

Early in the Souness era, Jock returned as a guest in the Thornton Suite hospitality area, but was politely asked to leave and shown the door. That, I think, would have hurt him more than anything and was something which angered those who had played under him at the time. Fortunately, once David Murray bought the club, Jock was welcomed at the ground, introduced to the fans before a match and they even held a testimonial dinner for him in that very same suite a few years before his death.

After his departure, Alex Totten became the latest caretaker boss, taking charge for a 2–1 defeat at Kilbowie, before Walter was announced as assistant manager to Souness. He took charge for another defeat against St Mirren at Love Street. Ironically, he would eventually take over from Graeme Souness at the same venue five years later.

Jock enjoyed socialising with his troops. On that Australian world tour he loved the fact that the boys would be together having a beer. He would join in, have a couple of halves and then leave you alone and go and do his own thing.

Of course, if you stepped out of line it was a different story and people rarely crossed him once, never mind a second time. We certainly saw the world under his management. The weirdest place we went to was Iraq where we faced the national team in two games and the Jordanians once.

The first hint we had that this trip, in March 1985, was going to be something special was when we had to sign a form stating that if we died on the trip our benefactors would get x amount.

We flew on Royal Jordanian Airlines on a plane that we discovered had recently been hijacked which wasn't exactly reassuring. On the flight, half the passengers got down on their knees in the aisle to pray to Allah, but there were a few guys who didn't move, the ones with the sub-machine guns, which wasn't exactly comforting at 30,000 feet.

When we arrived in Baghdad the runway lights went on for a few seconds to allow us to land then plunged us back into darkness. A blackout which was standard procedure while they were fighting a war with Iran.

I've been to a few strange places with Rangers and Hearts but this one was the mother of all trips. When we landed there were anti-aircraft guns everywhere. Everyone in the place looked like Saddam Hussein, and that was just the women. Jock of course was loving it. 'You're going to a war zone, boys. A wee bit of excitement for you,' he declared with relish.

That trip featured the best goal I've ever seen Ally score, and he's certainly got plenty to his credit. At the time he wasn't the hero he is now. The fact that he'd knocked Greigy back to sign for St Johnstone and then went to Sunderland, meant they had it in for him a bit and in those days he wasn't scoring just as regularly as he did in later seasons.

He was just over the halfway line, the ball bounced kindly for him and he drilled a volley nearly fifty yards into the top corner. He just couldn't believe it had gone in and neither could we.

The Republican Guard, Saddam's élite troops, made up the crowd and they showed their appreciation or displeasure by letting off a volley of automatic gunfire. It was without doubt the craziest atmosphere I've ever played in and only Jock could have organised such a trip.

The Australian trip was just as daunting. We stopped off at Singapore on our way to games in Melbourne and Perth. We had been travelling for 24 hours and were absolutely knackered when we eventually arrived at five in the morning. Then Jock had one of his brainwaves.

'Get to your beds. Get an hour's sleep, then we'll have breakfast and train. That'll get rid of your jet lag.'

So an hour or so later we were wiping the sleep from our eyes, got our training gear on and headed for a training pitch near the hotel, fully expecting a light warm-up and then back to bed. Instead he put us through one of the hardest training sessions I've ever had in my life. It made Gullane look like a picnic.

On the plus side, the big man could always take a joke, in its proper time and place of course.

During the trip one of Jock's cronies who was along for the ride, got hold of his passport and after a few beers let slip that his full name was John Bauchus Wallace. For the next couple of days we wound him up at every opportunity. 'Haw, Bauchus,' would be the shout.

'Who said that?' he'd demand. Then his mate would get a clout. 'You told them my middle name' he growled. 'I'll get you for that.'

Then there was the time we played a series of games in America. On the way to Los Angeles we crossed a couple of time zones and lost a day. Again it was time for the famous jet-lag cure and he had us running up and down Venice Beach.

As you can see beaches and sand played a big part in our lives at that time and for me sharing with Nicky 'the Fish' Walker it was even worse. All Nicky ever wanted to do, no matter where we were in the world, was go for a swim. In Australia the lure of Bondi Beach proved to be too much and he dragged me down there to join him.

Now it's maybe a great place in the summer, but this was an Aussie winter. The drizzle was rolling off the taxi window on the way and when we arrived it was absolutely freezing. Needless to say nobody else was daft enough even to think of going swimming at that time.

Sharks, huge breakers and the cold actually turned us into a tourist attraction. The locals were extremely curious, especially when Nicky thought it would be a laugh to pull my trunks down in front of our growing audience and disappear with all my clothes. Fortunately it was that cold, there was nothing to embarrass me.

As the postcards piled up on my mum and dad's mantlepiece, we took in New Zealand and Hawaii too.

Now Jock was also brilliant for letting you relax on tour, although he had a strict rule of no drinking in transit.

Ally had fallen foul of the big man before we even left Britain when the ground rules were laid down. Coisty disappeared at Heathrow and when Jock finally tracked him down he gave him a severe dressing down.

'I'm going to send you back up the road right now,' he threatened. 'This is a world tour. We're away for six weeks. You do exactly what I tell you, we all stick together and muck in,' he growled, ensuring a shaken Ally was on his best behaviour for the rest of the trip.

But he wasn't the only one to take some stick. Alex Totten, who was a great coach and a good manager was in charge of travel arrangements when we prepared to leave for America late one night. 'I'm just going to get all the boys together,' he told Jock at 11 in the morning

'Love to see it,' replied Jock slapping him on the back and handing him some cash to buy all the boys a drink. By two o'clock in the afternoon, the boys were half cut, but Jock was still quite happy, 'Good to see the boys enjoying themselves,' he said.

By four o'clock, having to be at the airport at seven, it was 'still here lads?' By five we were checking in at the airport and Alex headed straight for the bar at which point Jock had had enough. 'Alex, what have I told you. No drinking in transit!' he yelled.

We made 26 flights and played a lot of matches during the tour and even though the club must have made a few quid out of it, by the time we reached our last port of call, Toronto, we were all knackered.

But Jock was always a man for meeting the fans everywhere we went and at 11 a.m. we were off to another supporters' club and spent all day there. We met a lot of good people and the beer was flowing, but to be honest, I think we would have preferred to relax in the sun. In the end, we were glad to get back to pre-season for a rest!

If there were plenty of laughs on tour there were still some to be had at Ibrox, like the famous punch-up in the centre circle between Ally McCoist and Sandy Clark after he moved to Hearts.

It had been a typically physical match, a real high-tension affair when two players clashed in the middle of the park. Every now and again everyone else decides to join in and as we stood over Walter Kidd and Dougie Bell on the ground, Ally appeared on the scene and belted Sandy with a right hook.

It was red cards all round, but not as red as their faces afterwards as the two of them were good friends during and after their Ibrox days. It was later claimed that he was simply trying to improve on Sandy's good looks, but I don't think it made much of a difference.

Coisty is a genuinely nice guy which is why he's so popular, but he does have a habit of bottling up his emotions which is inevitable when you're in the spotlight so often. He lets things pass 99 per cent of the time, but like everyone he does lose his temper now and again.

He was under pressure to prove himself in his early days at Ibrox, then he was under pressure to keep his place during Souness's era. Then finally he's under pressure to improve on all the records he's already set, so things do get to him from time to time.

I've seen him threaten to hit someone on the training ground a few times and on one occasion he realised he was so angry he simply walked off the training pitch and back to the dressing-room to cool off which was the best thing he could have done.

It happens to everyone from time to time, especially at training. I've vented my own frustrations on some poor wee Mitre size 5 sometimes, booting it all round the park, but sometimes if you've got some big games coming up and things aren't going your way that's the way it goes.

Another wild man on the park at least was the fearsome Gregor Stevens. He made Tom Forsyth look soft at times. He was a real gentleman off the park and being a centre-half he obviously helped me a lot too and was very generous with his time.

During the game, it was a different matter. A real psycho look would appear, the red mist would descend, he'd lose his temper and then be heading for an early bath. He was eventually banned for six months after his fifth red card and left the club not long after. But I always felt people concentrated on the wild side of him and underrated him as a player. He had good feet and was good in the air for his size and did a great job for the club.

As I've said, Gregor and the rest of us would have run through a brick wall for Jock and the jersey, but sometimes that just isn't enough and we were unable to help him emulate his past glories.

This book was being written just as the tragic news came of the big man's untimely death, which was a huge shock to me and to countless team-mates, Rangers fans and everyone who'd ever met him. It's terrible to think that he's gone, obviously especially for his family, but he'll always be fondly remembered by Rangers fans and every single player who had the good fortune to be picked for one of his teams.

5

ORDER OF THE BOOT

The mad grin on Terry Butcher's face said it all! Down to ten men with just over 30 minutes on the clock in a crunch title decider with half of the Old and New Firms desperate to stop us, and we were 1–0 up!

The big man had got on the end of a Davie Cooper free-kick to score only his second goal of the season and we were on our way.

Losing our player-manager shortly before and then an equaliser from Brian Irvine were certainly setbacks, but after Terry's goal we were within touching distance of the Premier title for the first time in nine years.

It meant so much to the players and to the fans. When the final whistle went the fans invaded, and, not being used to such celebrations, I was a bit slower than some to head for the tunnel. Before I knew it someone had stolen the shirt off my back, literally! There was a mass of blue-and-white clad bodies on the Pittodrie pitch and every one was going mental. They were grabbing my hair, kissing me and before I knew it the strip was gone. Seconds later I was minus a pair of boots as well.

When I finally battled my way to the dressing-room I just sat there. I couldn't believe how it had happened, neither could the rest of the lads, but really we didn't care. It was a fantastic afternoon and one that will stick in the minds of all the players who were there.

A couple of years later I met of couple of Gers fans at a function who proudly admitted that it was them who stole my boots.

'We were drinking lager out of them all night, Dave, it was some party,' they told me.

Well, rather you than me lads!

Coisty suffered similar treatment and lost a gold chain which was ripped off, but at least he got it back when the fan in question's mother got hold of his address and posted it on.

All I was left wearing was my top. It was pure panic for the players. You just couldn't move and it was really claustrophobic. Shorts off, shinguards away. I was one of last ones back into dressing-room about half an hour after the game.

Alastair Hood suggested a lap of honour. 'Fine, I'd love to, but somebody better get me a pair of shorts.'

After we left Pittodrie, we stopped off for a well-deserved carry-out and swilled champagne all the way down to Dunblane. Terry, Chris, Rita Butcher, Sarah Woods, Donna and I went for a meal and then on to a disco in Stirling. We were understandably blitzed. We couldn't believe, after all we'd been through, that we'd finally done it.

It was a lot more emotional that time than on the other two occasions I've been privileged to win the league championship with Rangers. In the end we partied till dawn with Big Tel in top form.

He was a tremendous player and model professional who mixed equally well with his team-mates and the management. We ended up good friends and were out together virtually every weekend. An imposing figure, he's someone I'll always respect. He could be a real hard man but a genuine big guy and his influence that season and in ones to follow was immense.

Falkirk of course did us a real favour beating Celtic at Parkhead that day, but those two Tayside triumphs did the trick and we were celebrating after the Tannadice game.

At Pittodrie Terry scoring so early really helped and even though we were down to ten men and Brian Irvine equalised it turned into a stalemate after that and we were never going to lose it.

We collected the trophy in front of a full house at Ibrox the following week. A third-minute goal from Robert Fleck ensured we finished on a high against Cup finalists St Mirren. The result didn't matter, just the celebrations – and the fans loved every minute. But it was nothing compared to the madness of the previous Saturday when Big Tel's goal clinched the championship.

MacWoods MacButcher and MacRoberts as the English lads specially made T-shirts proclaimed, had a ball. They had tasted success in their first season at Rangers, but for other players at the club, including myself and Coisty, who had waited so long for the title to come back to Ibrox it meant even more.

It's hard, particularly for younger Rangers fans to understand in these days of Champions' Leagues and multi-million pound foreign stars at Ibrox with the coveted nine-in-a-row within touching distance, just how much that league win meant to everyone connected with Rangers after being starved of success for so many years.

I don't think even Graeme and Walter dreamed that they might pull it off in their first season, but I think the players had a gut feeling right from the first whistle at Easter Road that season, that we had the potential to bring back the championship trophy to Ibrox.

In Big Jock and John Greig's time we picked up a couple of League Cups and recorded some famous Old Firm victories, but for both of them, and the fans, with Celtic's domination in the late '60s and early '70s, flying the league flag over Ibrox again was *the* most important thing. Ultimately, even though Jock and John had both been involved in treble-winning seasons, 1976 and 1978, their failure to recapture the title cost them their jobs.

Following a clear-out at boardroom level, Lawrence Marlborough, grandson of the famous Rangers chairman John Lawrence, appointed David Holmes as Ibrox supremo. Holmes' masterstroke, bringing the former, Middlesbrough, Liverpool, Sampdoria and Scotland midfield maestro, Graeme Souness, sent shockwaves through Scottish football.

A decade later I still don't think people appreciate just what this meant for the Scottish game and how Souness dragged the standards up by the bootlaces.

The first indication that he wasn't going to play by the rules was the dramatic signings of England internationalists Terry Butcher and Chris Woods. Suddenly every player at Ibrox was looking over their shoulders as the transfer rumours flew and Souness and Smith set about building a team capable of winning the League.

I decided there and then that I wanted to be part of it. I got off to a good start under Walter by scoring the goal against Motherwell in our final league game that guaranteed us a UEFA Cup place the following season.

Afterwards Walter had a quiet word with me and said, 'I've told Graeme all about you and you're one of the players he wants to keep.'

It was a real weight off my mind and it was good of Walter to reassure me so early on. It stopped me worrying throughout the close season whether or not I'd be on my way. Then again, as I get older and more cynical, it has crossed my mind that maybe he told all of us the same thing.

Graeme duly arrived, sporting a sun tan honed on the Italian riviera and during the World Cup in Mexico, and made a huge impression. If nothing else he looked the part, he looked like a man of stature, immaculately dressed and very laid back. The smooth image was dented a bit as he went round the dressing-room introducing himself and shaking hands with the squad until he reached former Scotland team-mate Derek Johnstone.

'All right, Champagne Charlie,' said the big man with a huge grin, which brought a thin smile from Souness, even though it had been a nickname he'd worked hard for, especially in his days on Teesside.

Graeme was a very passionate man in everything he did, but he didn't apply the same logic to Old Firm derbies. Ironically, the first trophy he won at Ibrox was the Glasgow Cup – beating Celtic in the final. Even though it's supposedly a local competition, it's played at Hampden and means as much to the punters as any other; and it was still a trophy, which was a great start.

To me, Rangers and Celtic games were the most important in the world, but initially, Graeme refused to subscribe to this and reckoned that in terms of points, you got the same for beating Partick Thistle as you did for winning against Celtic.

Similarly, you could go through the entire season losing to Celtic and still win the League as long as other people were taking points off them, and that was always the main objective.

The fans, needless to say, felt the reverse.

This wasn't the only shake-up. He changed the way players thought as well and was a lot more professional in his approach to matches, treating every game the same way.

I have to say it was a very educational year for me. The European and Anfield influence on his tactics and coaching were there for all to see on the training ground.

But even though it was hard work and the pressures of wearing the blue jersey were even greater, it was fun. There was a lot of emphasis on warm-ups and stretching and even the five-a-side games were

Donna McPherson with Terry
Butcher and Chris Woods' wife,
Sarah, at the players' end-of-sea-
son dance in 1987.

Back in Blue: shortly after
signing for Rangers again.

Ally and Dave
in Canada
during
Scotland's
warm-up North
American tour.

The celebrations begin at Broomfield after winning the league title
against Airdrie.

Ya Beauty! Another Ibrox strike in Dave's second spell there.

A jubilant team after clinching the treble against Aberdeen in May 1993.

Treble Champs: Ally and Allison McCoist with Donna and Dave at the treble-winning end-of-season dance.

In action against Marseille in the Champions' League 1993.

Back at Hearts once again.

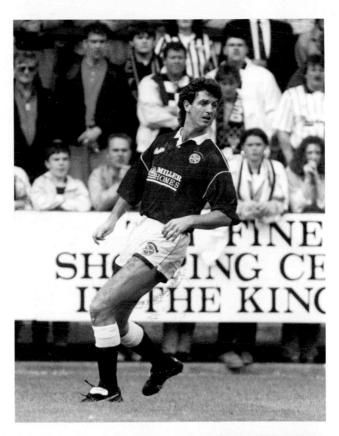

A trophy at Tynecastle - even though it belongs to world snooker champion and Jambo, Stephen Hendry.

Dave at the launch of the
Hearts' tartan.

Dave and Donna at home.

Hearty Boys! Dave
and son Christopher.

fantastic. They were ten times faster than a match, but if you could play in them and adjust to the pace, you'd be fit enough for a Saturday – that was where you got your fitness.

Thanks to the English invasion with Woodsy, Big Terry, Colin West and the guys that followed, it was England v Scotland most days and it made *Braveheart* look tame. Coisty, of course, was our answer to Mel Gibson, only Mel's smaller.

The Scots players had plenty to prove, but sometimes you got the feeling that no matter how much talent you had and how much you raised your game and slogged your guts out for Graeme, he still wouldn't rate you. You always felt secure with Jock and John, but Souness had the knack of making you feel you weren't good enough, no matter what you did.

I didn't like the way he referred to a lot of homegrown players as 'you Jocks', which depending on the context, isn't the most complimentary label. Having played all his career in England, he obviously didn't regard himself as one, even though he played 54 times for his country.

Ironically, the one man at Ibrox who turned out to be a bigger 'Jock' than anyone was England legend Terry Butcher who has claimed honorary Scots status and settled with his family in Stirlingshire. Terry was an inspirational captain and was a major figure in our success that year.

Souness didn't have the knowledge of the Scottish game that previous bosses had, but he didn't need to – he had Walter.

After a solid playing career with Dumbarton and Dundee United, where he played in the '70s Cup final team alongside Archie Knox, Walter had become involved on the coaching side of things at Tannadice as quickly as possible.

If Graeme had learned under the likes of the irreplaceable Bill Shankly, Walter had a good apprenticeship under Jim McLean, who had ruled Tannadice with an iron fist for years.

Ironically, McLean, whose brother Tommy was caretaker boss at Ibrox for a brief spell, had previously been offered the Ibrox hotseat in the wake of John Greig's departure and, along with Aberdeen boss Alex Ferguson, had refused it – something which would have been unthinkable for any manager in the past.

Walter and Graeme had a good cop-bad cop kind of relationship with the players. Walter always got on well with the squad, and was able to turn a blind eye to some of the high jinks, while Graeme had the reputation for being stricter in terms of discipline. Even in those early days, we realised there could only be one boss and it wasn't a good idea to cross him.

Equally, on a one-to-one basis, Graeme could be a charming and funny guy and most of the things he had forbidden players to do he'd done himself at some point, so as long as it wasn't getting in the way of your football there were no real problems.

It didn't matter anyway, he wasn't there to make friends – just to turn Rangers around.

The most visible sign of the impact he'd made was when the fans came flooding back. In the bad old days, with the usual exception of Old Firm games, even though we were getting crowds of 15,000, which would be quite respectable for other teams, figures like that made Ibrox look empty. At last, we were playing to a full house again and that in itself was brilliant for all the players.

A 2–0 defeat against Spurs in an end-of-season friendly on 6 April 1986 in front of just 12,600 fans was the last straw for the Ibrox board. Jock himself said afterwards that the performance was a 'disgrace' and that the team had 'let the fans down'. But no one could have known that two days later, the World Cup skipper who had tasted European success with Liverpool, would be in charge having knocked back an offer from Spurs and completed a £300,000 move.

And for our next friendly match, 36,000 turned out to watch us against Bayern Munich!

Throughout the summer the hype built up until the new player-manager's debut, the first league match of the season against Hibs at Easter Road got off to an explosive start.

The tension was high with the players wanting to prove to their new boss that they could do the job. And of course, even before Souness's arrival, there had always been a bit of jealousy as we were by now the highest earners in Scottish football.

When he arrived the money was even better, but what really fired up opposing teams, not just Hibs, was the arrogance that rubbed off on us. Every player, with the exception of Alan Rough ended up getting booked and Souness was red carded for a tackle on George McCluskey which started a pitched battle.

It was some start and there was plenty more controversy to come as we charged towards the title and just as dramatic an end to the season nine months later.

As I've said, no one apart from the players thought we could do it, but we knew from the word go that it was within our grasp.

After that Hibs game, Graeme was immediately under fire and it intensified when we lost 3–2 to Dundee United after being 2–0 up. There was a lot of gloating going on after that, but even though we lost we had played brilliantly for 80 minutes and we realised if we continued to play like that the League was there for the taking.

Tel was just back from the World Cup and I found I could learn just by watching him in action. I got on really well with the big man on and off the park and I thought we made a good combination. He was a big dominant centre-half, who was good in the air, but had great skill as well.

Socially it was a brilliant year and I had a great time with the likes of Terry and Chris who both stayed in Dunblane.

Because of the battle in that first game, I was suspended for the League Cup final. As well as being booked, the SFA in their usual wisdom handed out another yellow card to every player as well.

I already had a medal from the previous March when we'd won the trophy under Jock, but when the competition was switched to its successful October slot, I found myself with another one, even though I had to watch from the stand.

Celtic were three points clear in the League at the time and even though a Durranty goal had given us victory in the first league clash, with Souness injured and me suspended, we were the underdogs.

But Ian was the hero again beating Pat Bonner after a Derek Ferguson free-kick. Brian McClair equalised, but with six minutes to go Big Tel was hauled down by Roy Aitken and Davie Cooper converted the spot kick.

There was more controversy as Mo Johnston was stupidly red-carded for headbutting Stuart Munro, but when the final whistle went, we had our first taste of victory under our new management.

As the celebrations began, Souness handed me a medal as a thank you for my efforts in playing every tie on the way to Hampden. At first I was stunned, but that soon changed to delight as I joined in the party with the rest of the lads. It was the second time in a relatively short career that I'd been given a medal even though I hadn't played in the match. It's always nicer to have won it on the day, but it was some consolation for the agony of missing out on the big day. I had played in all the previous rounds, but it was still a big blow; the team won it without me and nothing can change that.

Graeme had also made me feel a part of the build-up, inviting me down to the Marine Hotel in Troon where I had more than a couple of beers with trainer Phil Boersma to cheer me up.

The celebrations afterwards were great, until the McPherson, McCoist and Durrant party decided to do their celebrating on top of the table. I ended up with an even sorer head than I would have had after misjudging the distance to the roof and sticking my head through the suspended ceiling. Coisty and Durrant, of course, collapsed with laughter.

Souness didn't do a lot of shouting on the pitch, but he was a great player with a fine touch and a superb passer of the ball. Even though the game in Scotland was a lot faster than he was used to, he adapted very quickly. He was very arrogant and could dish out a fair bit of stick when he needed to – but he could take it as well. He was a great encouragement to all around him on the pitch and a great role model for any young player. Winning the European Cup with Liverpool made him a bit special. He didn't get on too well with the SFA establishment and that eventually played a part in his decision to take the Liverpool job

One big low of the season came just after that Hibs match when I was sent off against Aberdeen for clattering Davie Dodds, who was later to become first-team coach at Rangers. Doddsie was back marking me at a set-piece and even though he was never a dirty player he always gave you a rough time. His elbows didn't stay by his sides too often. As we waited for the ball to come in he was niggling away, tugging my jersey and eventually I just snapped. I told him where to go and brought my elbow up. I swear I didn't mean to catch him right on the bridge of the nose, but even though I was quick to protest my innocence when I saw the linesman watching the whole thing, the fact that Davie was lying on the deck with blood all over his face didn't help my cause.

It was one of the longest walks I've ever taken from the far corner of Pittodrie diagonally into the corner where the tunnel is. I was even more upset when I glanced across to where Graeme Souness was sitting and spotted that he was looking extremely unchuffed.

In true Terry Butcher fashion, I booted the dressing-room door in, sent a few objects flying and then shed some tears of pure frustration.

Afterwards, Souness was spot on when he told me 'It was your own fault. You weren't having a good game and you let it get the better of you. You might not play well all the time, but you've got to learn to handle the fact that an opponent is getting the better of you. Take a deep breath and remember that next time you'll be the one who comes out on top.'

He was absolutely right, but it didn't stop him getting sent off against the Dons in that climactic title-winning match.

It wasn't a great period all round for me. I was really gutted to miss the Cup final, although getting the medal took some of the sting out of it. Those disciplinary points on the first day of the season were having an effect and we did suffer from suspensions, but even though Graeme himself was guilty of going over the top sometimes, eventually things settled down.

Graeme was a good motivator. He didn't say a lot in the dressing-room before a game, but he managed to get everyone psyched up quite easily.

When the battle of Easter Road erupted, one of the plus points was that he was pleased that when the trouble started we all piled in literally team-handed. That ability to fight for each other and the team spirit we showed during our first competitive game together delighted him. Obviously we had to cut out the dirty stuff, but a lot of the more physical confrontations weren't down to us.

Even during our barren years in the doldrums, we were still the side everyone wanted to beat and the club everyone loved to hate. When Souness arrived and our own confidence, arrogance even, grew as his influence rubbed off, they *really* hated us.

The club's reputation, size and past glories all came into it, but I have to say that jealousy on the part of other pros also played its part. Davie Cooper had become the first Ibrox player to get a signing-on fee when he dug his heels in and broke the previously empty mould. But when Souness took over higher wages, bonuses and perks became the norm.

Before Terry and the rest of the English gang arrived, I was the highest paid player at Ibrox on a princely sum of £300 a week. There was a set wage structure and not a penny more.

When Graeme arrived we knew it had taken big bucks to lure top stars from south of the border to Govan and I think a few of us said to ourselves, 'Hang on a minute, we're doing the same job, playing in the same team, but we're still getting paid at the old rate.'

After preparing what I thought was a good case, I walked into Graeme's office and demanded a pay rise.

'All right, I'll give you £400,' he replied, which stopped me dead in my tracks.

'Hang on, I haven't even haggled here,' I thought. 'What do you mean £400, I only wanted £350.'

That more or less summed up the new regime. I didn't want to tell him that I would probably have settled for £25, but when I came out of his office I was on cloud nine. He was brilliant in that respect; it was also a boost that he thought you were worth it.

I had my ups and downs with Graeme and disagreed with certain views he held and things he did, but I had a lot of respect for him as a boss and he definitely did a lot for me.

David Murray has to take a lot of credit for everything he's done at Ibrox since he took over in 1988.

But for me, David Holmes deserves far more plaudits than he got either at the time or since. He was a very shrewd and tough businessman, but also a really nice man and he was as delighted as the rest of us in the dressing-room as the title-winning party started. Without him there would have been no Souness. Without Souness, no success and probably no David Murray either, though Ayr United might have won the European Cup by now!

Holmes and Souness had a lot of hard decisions to take, including letting go the old guard who had served Rangers so well in previous glory years. But, as I was to find out to my cost, right or wrong, neither was scared to make a decision.

The League was a big bonus that year, but with his own glories in the European Cup whetting his appetite, Graeme was always keen for us to make our mark in Europe that year. He desperately wanted to join Willie Waddell in bringing European success back to Ibrox, but like the Scottish Cup, it was something that was always out of his grasp.

I've got quite a good record in Europe. After beating Ilves Tampere, who had given us a hard game in Finland, I got on the scoresheet when we beat Boavista of Portugal.

I scored 12 goals in all that season, which is a fair total for a central defender and I'm happy to say a few of them came in vital league matches.

For me, the League was virtually won in March, 17 and 21, when we come out on top in two crucial trips to Tayside. We faced Dundee, who have been something of a bogey team for Rangers over the years, and United, who had already beaten us that season, in swift succession.

We knew that draws wouldn't be good enough from then on in, as Celtic were piling on the pressure and snapping at our heels. But on the night, playing at Dens Park in the rearranged fixture, we were nothing short of brilliant. We gave one of the best performances of the season and ran out 4–0 winners thanks to a double from Coisty, one from Robert Fleck and a quality strike from yours truly.

On the Saturday we faced another tough test against a Dundee United side who had already proved that, on top form, they were a match for anyone. I have to confess I had a horrible game. Virtually the whole match passed me by and I didn't get a sniff of the ball until I popped up to score the only goal of the game. Modesty should prevail, but I have to say it was one of my best goals. Davie Cooper swung in a free-kick from the right and even though the penalty box was like Sauchiehall Street on a Saturday afternoon I sent a deft flick with my head into the corner of the net – and yes, I did mean it!

Even though my overall performance wasn't up to scratch I found myself man of the match in the *Sunday Mail* Starcheck!

Those two results gave us a taste of what could be and especially being away from home, I would say that they won us the League. The campaign was at a crucial stage, but we all believed we could go all the way that Saturday night if we kept our nerve and our form.

Another critical result was a 5–2 win over Hearts the previous month. Even now Tynecastle is a tough place for Rangers to go, but that was a real morale-booster, especially for Robert Fleck who grabbed a hat-trick including a great overhead kick. Graeme Souness was criticised for buying success, but with the time he had available he had to bring in the best players he could. People who criticised him for that often forgot that guys like Ian Durrant, Flecky, Derek Ferguson and in later years John Spencer, Charlie Miller and Gary McSwegan all came through the ranks to the first team.

That Tynecastle trip was the occasion of the famous incident Robbo mentioned in his foreword where he conned his way to a penalty kick.

I was running back and he tripped me up – my wee pal! Unbelievably the ref awarded Hearts the free-kick, they quickly played it to Robbo, Graeme Roberts tripped him, down he went again and somehow he recovered in time to score with the penalty.

That was the first time Hearts had lost at Tynecastle in over 18 months and it was just what we needed after our previous match, against Hamilton.

Even now that Scottish Cup tie is still an infamous night. Graeme always maintained that the League was his number one priority, but he wanted to do well in the Scottish Cup too, and he certainly expected us to beat Hamilton at home, but it wasn't to be. I was most gutted for Woodsy. He had been performing brilliantly and set a new British shut-out record during the game, only to see it snatched away minutes later. But Chris was brilliant afterwards.

'I wanted to keep the record going, but I had to lose one sometime. I'm hardly going to blame you for it,' he shrugged.

We took some unbelievable flak for that defeat and all the old comparisons with the club's shock exit against Berwick Rangers twenty years before were dragged up.

Souness, I regret to say was not as magnanimous in defeat as Chris and called me a rude name! Mind you I'm in good company – he had a few choice names for the others, too.

After a good bit of cursing, the full spiel went along the lines of 'You've let yourself and the team down . . .'

I didn't need telling. I felt bad enough already, but it was just a case of him taking his frustration out on me. I wasn't one of his signings, so he singled me out and had a go. Over the season I suppose he treated us all pretty fair, but the Scots lads seemed to take more stick than most and I can remember him saying at one stage, 'You Jocks have caused me nothing but trouble.'

Without attempting to make any excuses for my own lapse in concentration, it was just one of those games. Dave McKellar in the

Hamilton goal must have had glue on his gloves as he caught everything and played an absolute blinder. I'm not having a go at our strikers for not scoring – I missed a few chances myself. Even a side like Rangers has off nights and there'll be more to come in the future.

A free-kick came over Souness's head which I had expected him to get and the next thing I knew it was under my foot and Adrian Sprott nipped in to score.

To be fair to Souness, he didn't blame me in the press. He liked to keep things within the four walls of the dressing-room. Mind you, I tried to blame him, I thought he had the ball covered, but passing the buck to the player-manager was never a sound option.

I was absolutely slaughtered, but I bit my tongue and showed him the respect he was due as manager, even if I totally disagreed with most of it. At the end of the day he never dropped me. I played right-back, centre-half and right midfield and turned out every week, but always knowing at the back of my mind that if he could have found a replacement for me I'd be on my way.

Being a defender is a real no-win situation. You're always in the front line for any flak when things go wrong, but last to get any plaudits. I played out of position in a number of games that season and got precious little credit for it. Fans would say that they didn't think you looked right in that position. I know! But you've just got to give it your best shot.

Eventually after that league match against St Mirren, my celebrations were short-lived. The final nail in the coffin was our trip to Tel Aviv to play the Israel B team. I'm a bad flyer and Ally Dawson wasn't the greatest traveller either, so during the marathon trip both of us got absolutely wrecked on the plane. Souness wasn't best pleased with either of us.

If you look at the team list for that game, you'll see Substitutes: McPherson, Dawson.

Looking back, that was the first inkling I had that maybe I wouldn't be part of things the following season and the writing was on the wall, but at the time I put it down to our mile-high binge and happily headed off on holiday with Donna, Chris Woods and his wife Sarah and our families. We had a great trip until we arrived back at Glasgow airport. Donna's dad picked us up.

'Have you seen the papers?' he asked. 'No, I don't read them on holiday,' I replied.

'You're going to Hearts,' he said, bringing my world crashing round about me with one sentence.

6

MAROONED

It turned out to be spot on. Donna's dad had initially told me it was a £400,000 deal with Hugh Burns as the main part of it, but it turned out to be the other way round.

I was sitting at home still stunned by the newspaper reports when I got a call from Graeme Souness.

'We've had an offer from Hearts for you . . . I think you should take it,' he said simply.

'I was a bit disappointed to see it in the papers first,' I told him, but he simply repeated that he thought I should go and that was that.

I was bitter then and I'm still bitter. I had played a part in the club's first major success in nine years and genuinely believed my future lay there. When you're that age you think you'll be there for ever, so it was a total bombshell. I would rather he had told me to my face that he didn't fancy me and was going to sell me, but he never did that.

I called Walter the next day to find out what was going on, but again he was to the point.

'Hearts have made an offer and Graeme wants to sell you. He thinks that you'll be a good player in the long term, but he wants success immediately. He can't wait for you to mature to your full potential.'

'Well, I don't agree with him and I'm not leaving until I get something from the club,' I said, trying to dig my heels in.

'Rangers don't pay players to leave,' said Watty, although eventually something was sorted out to compensate me for ripping up my contract. But a few quid was no compensation after 222 first-team appearances, 26 goals, a league championship and two League Cup medals, I was on my way.

I'm not ashamed to admit I was in tears the day I walked out of the main door at Ibrox with my boots in my hand. Having been so used to going through that imposing entrance and into the hallowed Ibrox dressing-rooms I was absolutely gutted, particularly as I didn't get the chance to say goodbye to anyone, though I did speak to Terry and Coisty on the phone and neither of them could believe it.

For any player to leave Ibrox and not be part of it any more is hard, even guys from down south who have only been there for a season, and it took me a long time to get used to it.

I think Rangers made a mistake and might even have come to regret their decision the following season when they lost out to Celtic in the League and struggled to replace Big Terry after he broke his leg.

After the bombshell news that Rangers were ready to sell me, there came a real day of reckoning. I went for a drive with Donna and we stopped at the seaside just outside Largs.

I've never been scared to make a decision, but this one was going to affect my whole future and I couldn't afford to get it wrong. I spent ten minutes on my own trying to work out whether it was going to be better to stay and fight and maybe be messed about and spend most of my time in the reserves or to go and make a fresh start.

After a lot of soul-searching, all the conflicting thoughts and fears that had been tearing me apart resolved themselves.

I made up my mind and told Donna: 'I'm going to sign for Hearts, but I'll be back at Ibrox some day and prove that they made a mistake.'

I only half believed it at the time, but that's exactly how it turned out.

The decision to leave Ibrox just as the club finally turned its fortunes round and marched towards a new era of domination was a terrible one. But now I realise it was definitely the right one. I knew that I would be good enough to go back although I didn't know for certain that I would ever get the chance again. I was absolutely devastated to find out they wanted rid of me. I honestly thought my future lay there. But once I had agreed to talk to Hearts and met Alex, Sandy and the chairman, they were superb and made it easy. They cheered me up immediately. Wallace told me that I would play for

Scotland and eventually I could make a bigger move anyway. Alex revealed he had been watching me all season and had actually made a bid at Christmas which I'd never been told about.

I could have said no and stayed to fight for my place at Ibrox, but Wallace was brilliant. He honestly knew how I felt and understood everything I was going through.

'Don't worry, you're wanted here,' he told me. 'A lot of people look on it as a step down, but it's really a step sideways and you can go back up.'

A lot has been said about Wallace Mercer, mostly by Wallace himself, but I loved my first spell at Tynecastle under him. I thought he was great and he really looked after me when I first signed.

7

TAKING HEART

Once I had made up my mind, I handled the transfer myself. The financial details were settled easily and we shook hands on a deal at Wallace's Edinburgh home.

I felt a part of things at Tynecastle from the word go and I had a great relationship with the chairman and Alex, or Doddy, as he's known to one and all. I was made club captain, involved in a lot of decisions and given some responsibility. I like to think I did my best to repay him for that.

Doddy did a magnificent job for Hearts and built up a great side with a great team spirit. I settled well when I first moved there. I already knew a lot of the players which helped, and my first games for Hearts were on a pre-season trip to Germany where any doubt I had about going there just evaporated.

I took a shine to Doddy. I thought he was a great manager and very easy to get along with, as was Sandy.

Craig Levein and I got to know each other when we became roommates on that trip, especially when we went shopping together for a few bottles of plonk to take home.

That evening we started telling a few stories about what it was like playing with Rangers and Hearts and then I suggested we open one of the bottles and have a couple of glasses of wine. Of course, it didn't end there. The banter started flying and things got more hilarious by the glass. In the early hours of the morning someone knocked on the ceiling for us to quieten down, but our reply was unprintable. Eventually about 3 a.m. the door went and it was Doddy with a face like thunder. I thought to myself, 'Great. I'm really making a great impression here getting caught on the bevvy on my first trip abroad with the club.'

'Do you want to come in,' I asked.

'Come in? With the racket you two are making? You're joking,' said Doddy. 'Get yourself up to my room right now.'

With Craig sniggering behind me, Doddy led us upstairs with me fearing a fine or a bollocking was on the cards. Instead he told us, 'Next time you have a party, I want an invite. Now get your arses back down there and get another bottle opened.'

Three bottles later we headed back downstairs bleary eyed, having had an even better laugh with Alex and Walter Borthwick who had a few tales of their own to tell.

We weren't doing anything out of turn as we had played that afternoon, but he treated you with a bit of respect, not like a kid. That helped break the ice and I went on to enjoy my first season there.

My debut came against Falkirk at home on the opening day of the 1987–88 season and thankfully I got off to a winning start as we romped home 5–2.

I had played in a couple of pre-season friendlies, but you don't really get to know the players or how you're going to fit in until that first league match. I wasn't nervous, I've never been a nervous player, but I found it so strange to play in a competitive game and not have a Rangers jersey on or be playing at Ibrox. It took me the entire first 45 minutes to get used to the idea and if I'm honest, personally it wasn't the greatest of starts. No matter what I did I couldn't win a header or a tackle, but fortunately this was masked by the rest of the team's performance. Everyone else looked sharp and was buzzing about creating plenty of chances. Meanwhile I was wandering about glancing down at this strange maroon outfit I had acquired. But at least we got the points and got off to a flying start in the League.

Having played at youth international level and gone on holiday with Gary Mackay, Gordon Marshall, John Robertson and Dave Bowman, it made it easy for me to settle. That was one of the reasons I signed. And of course I already knew Alex, Sandy Jardine, Sandy Clark and Kenny Black from my Ibrox days.

Going back to Ibrox was another big obstacle. After so many years there, it felt really strange to be in the away dressing-room, but of course having been dumped by Rangers, I was determined to prove that they were wrong to have sold me. That first clash ended goalless and four days later I grabbed my first goal for Hearts in a 2–1 home win over Aberdeen.

The good start we'd made to the campaign continued when we thumped Falkirk 4–1 at Brockville the following Saturday.

I scored another three league goals for the Jambos in that opening season. Two against Dunfermline and I'm very happy to report, one against Rangers on 2 April when we won 2–1 at Ibrox, with Robbo grabbing the winner.

Honours were shared that season with two draws and a win apiece, but we still finished above Souness's men in the League, which was a source of great personal satisfaction to me, although I suspect that a big factor in their disappointing season was losing Terry Butcher with a broken leg.

They did dump us in the League Cup with doubles from McCoist and Durrant and a solitary goal from Robbo in September. There was more cup heartache when we blew our place in the Scottish Cup final after a late collapse against Celtic at Hampden.

One of the best weeks was when we played Aberdeen on the Saturday at home and beat them, beat United at Tannadice on the Wednesday and completed the hat-trick against Celtic the following Saturday. To get maximum points from three hard games was great.

Playing against Rangers was not without its problems and there have been several rumbles in the tunnel over the years. There was a big bust-up in March 1990 at Tynecastle. That stemmed from an earlier incident when there were four booked and Mark Walters was ordered off on 4 December 1989. We beat Rangers 2–1 and Souness reckoned I had got Mark his marching orders, which was wrong. The truth was, like any forward, his timing in the tackle wasn't the best and Mark used to dive in first and ask questions later. That time he caught me with a late challenge and, even though I rode the tackle, the ref decided enough was enough.

Afterwards there was a bit of argy bargy in the tunnel and Doddy who had a razor-sharp tongue was never slow to get a dig in, tore into Walter and Graeme letting them know in no uncertain terms to leave his players alone. Souness had a go and Doddy stuck up for me. When that happens the Rangers players stick up for their boss, just as we had done at the battle of Easter Road and vice versa for the Hearts players.

There was a rematch at Tynecastle in the New Year, but the Tynecastle tunnel is very tight and there are a lot of bodies in there after a game. There can be a fair bit of back chat and shouting and swearing, but usually it's handbags at five paces and doesn't come to much.

There's been a crackdown on that kind of thing in recent years, but sometimes managers are the worst. They're even more hyped up than the players and can get even more frustrated because they're not actually on the park, able to have an input. When that happens more often than not the players figure that they've got a free hand and steam in as well. I was always fired up for matches against Rangers and, of course, we all wanted to do well against Hibs; matches against Motherwell had that extra bit of dig in them too.

Those games always produced a lot of controversy and plenty of yellow and red cards. I had a running battle with Nick Cusack and was sent off for a tackle on him during one match. Walter Kidd also suffered a similar fate in bizarre circumstances.

He was chasing Steve Kirk down the wing trying to win the ball off him, when the Motherwell player slapped his thigh, which made a noise, and then took a dive. Hearing the noise and seeing the end result the referee sent him for an early bath, despite Walter's protests. Quite understandably he hated Kirk after that. Getting a fellow pro sent off is regarded as one of the worst things you can do. Andy Goram also had a few run-ins with the same player and isn't a fan either. I don't know how all this started, but even now there's that bit of niggle between the sides.

Doddy would always back his players to the hilt, but if he thought you were in the wrong he wasn't slow to let you know. Even though Alex is a nice guy, he's definitely no soft touch. He didn't let you get away with much, especially on the park. Just before I broke through to the international scene, we played Ayr United in a Cup tie. I modestly thought I had had a great game and scored a goal with a one–two and then finished with a header. It's always nice to hear the manager say you've done well, which was what I was expecting on this occasion, but instead Doddy made a beeline for me in the dressing-room and started telling me where I was going wrong.

'This incident in the corner in the first half, you were about here away from your man. You've got to be here,' he roared. 'Get f*****g tighter!'

I was nearly crying. I thought I'd had this flawless game, but here I was getting ripped to shreds. Afterwards I didn't mind too much as I realised he was only trying to help.

'The national team coach was watching the game. He picks up on things like that, you've got to get tighter,' he said again.

He was only giving me a hard time for my own good and eventually I did get my first Scotland cap. I was delighted that my efforts had been rewarded, but I hadn't done it on my own – Alex had played a big part in getting me there and I owe him for that.

The most memorable thing for me was the training Alex put us through. After Souness's Italian-influenced approach, with plenty of five-a-side games, it was a real shock to go back to the old Jock Wallace days. Alex was a huge fan of Jock's and believed the methods that had brought two trebles were good enough for his sides as well.

It was a very physical approach with a lot of running, morning and afternoon. He kept you going non-stop. It was incredibly hard and took me about three weeks to recover. Eventually you got used to it, but the first few days were absolute murder.

John Robertson, John Colquhoun and I have all left Hearts and then happily rejoined. One of the reasons for ending up back in the fold is that the club genuinely has a family atmosphere. Everybody who plays for the club feels a part of it and that has stayed the same no matter who's been in charge.

Not everybody would agree, but even though Wallace Mercer was a larger than life, autocratic figure, he could also relate to the players. He could tell you what he wanted for the club and where he wanted to take it. In general, everything he did was for the good of the club and he probably left at the right time, having done as much as he could.

There were the occasional brainstorms, like his takeover bid for Hibs. That was always going to be a non-starter, but Wallace was genuinely mystified and even hurt at the reaction. A lot of people don't realise just how great the rivalry is, or the depth of feeling both sets of fans have for their teams. In some ways it's even worse than the rivalry between the Old Firm in Glasgow, but Wallace was oblivious to this. He was horrified at what he'd stirred up after he started receiving death threats from both sets of fans, a Hands off Hibs campaign started and there were rallies at the Usher hall.

It was bedlam, but I could see the thinking that lay behind it. Like everything else, it was strictly business, but his attempt to be the Godfather of Edinburgh football was an offer the fans could refuse. The punters took it personally, while he explained it to me as simply a matter of supply and demand and basic football economics. Alone, neither side will ever enjoy the type of income in terms of sponsorship or gate money that the Old Firm commands. Together, if they could have buried nearly a century of rivalry, off and on the field, he reckoned there was a better chance of matching them.

A few Hearts players were upset about the proposals and John Robertson went as far as to speak out against it.

Robbo's an honest guy who believes in speaking his mind and I could understand that, but I still didn't think he was right publicly to disagree with the chairman. If you're a Hearts player and they're paying your wages, you have a kind of collective responsibility to toe the party line.

At the end of the day, it was never going to happen. Even if Wallace had been successful in his bid, the Hibs fans and probably a lot of Hearts fans would have stayed away and any Edinburgh United side would have been playing in front of an empty stadium.

It's something that's been suggested in Dundee as well where both clubs exist yards from each other, but again there's no danger of that ever happening either.

To me, the way forward for Scottish football is expansion with more clubs in the top division rather than integration with less teams. I'd like to see a 16-strong Premier Division up here and there's plenty of room for another four sides.

Apart from competitive matches, I've done my fair share of globetrotting for pre-season friendlies. Like any European trips, they're great for building team spirit and even though the football is serious there are plenty of laughs.

On one trip with Hearts under Doddy's command, we were in Spain and didn't put in a particularly good performance, which was understandable as there had been a lot of travelling and we were all knackered. Afterwards Doddy cornered Craig Levein.

'I've told you about passing the ball long instead of short,' he said. 'You made a short pass, we got caught out and they scored.'

'I passed it to Neil Berry,' Craig protested. 'It's not my fault if Neil hasn't got a good first touch and he gave the ball away.'

'Exactly!' Alex blasted. 'That's the reason I'm telling you not to pass it to him.'

Neil was looking slightly bemused by all this. We'd had a few drinks and it nearly came to blows but eventually things calmed down. The next morning Craig was sitting at breakfast and he eyed the boss warily as he approached our table.

'How are you and me getting on big man? Everything all right?' he asked, and that was it.

That was the great thing about Alex you could have almost a stand-up fight with him during an argument and the next morning he'd walk up and shake your hand and it was all forgotten. He never held any grudges and as long as you gave him a bit of respect, which we did, he gave you the same back.

On another occasion, we played in Romania. Normally we travel first class and get in and out as quickly as possible, but this was different. Firstly we had to fly to Gatwick to catch a Romanian Airlines plane, instead of going direct. I think there are 54 terminals there and of course we were number 54. When we were driven out on to the tarmac, we got a double shock. The first was the plane which was an old propeller job, and the second was the fact that the baggage was strewn all over the runway and we had to load it ourselves.

This took about an hour in the sweltering sunshine before we finally boarded the Russian-built Ilyushin, known in airline circles as an Illusion because no one could believe that it was going to get off the ground. I was seriously considering refusing to get on, but I was finally talked into it, knowing that these things had a nasty habit of dropping out of the sky and vanishing.

The next laugh was the safety procedure. No pull down oxygen masks here. No, instead the stewardess explained in broken English that the plan was that, if necessary, she would come round with a trolley and give everyone a shot. You didn't have to be a genius to work out that if the plane went into a dive there was no way she would get round any passengers.

The next stage of what was a less than magical mystery tour was a detour to Brussels to pick up a Belgian team. Seven hours later we couldn't believe that we'd made it alive to Bucharest, then had a further shock when we sampled the local fare.

At that stage of the season you need plenty of nosh, especially carbohydrates, but I was on the toilet for a week when we got home and the players were wasting away. Even the mineral water, normally a safer bet than the tap variety looked like dirty dish water and tasted just as bad. After returning to Scotland, we were supposed to fly to Valencia, but I couldn't get off the toilet seat never mind go to Spain.

That trip certainly took its toll and we were so ill-prepared for the season we had a terrible start to our league campaign and eventually it cost Alex his job.

There were more pre-season high jinks on a trip to Germany. It was a low-budget affair with a squad of around 20 crammed into a guest house. We had a nice training area, but we had to drive ourselves there every day in two orange minibuses.

This became a great source of entertainment every morning. It was like the RAC Rally through those country roads and, being a sensible driver myself, I wasn't prepared for Hugh Burns who drove like a maniac trying to ram us off the road. It was a miracle no one was killed. It was like something out of *Mad Max*, but a good time was had all the same.

Looking back at the stick the Aberdeen players took for breaking a curfew during their recent pre-season jaunt, I have to say I thought the treatment they got was over the top.

When you've been training hard and travelling for two weeks, you need a release. Most clubs allow you to have a drink on the last couple of nights and the curfew actually gets broken a lot. But it's never by any great deal of time and, as most of these places are so out of the way you're lucky if there's more than one pub anyway, the lads are usually just relaxing together.

Anyway judging by the thumping they gave us at Pittodrie at the start of the season it didn't do them any harm. I have to admit any sympathy I might have felt disappeared that afternoon.

Returning to those days under Doddy, I was really pleased to be awarded the captaincy in July 1989. Gary Mackay went to see the boss and asked if he could give it up. Being a lifelong Jambo meant there was even more pressure on him, so it was beneficial for him and the team for him to relinquish the captain's armband.

Alex approached me and I didn't have to think twice. It was a great honour and, after hitting rock bottom, just what I needed to rebuild my self-esteem and career. To have the added responsibility, which I knew I could handle, was great.

Alex had built a good squad of professionals. There has always been a strong contingent of ex-Ibrox stars, including Sandy and Alex, Hugh Burns, Iain Ferguson, Cammy Fraser, Willie Johnston, Jim Denny, Colin McAdam, Billy McKay, Gregor Stevens and Kenny Black. At that time Sandy Clark was doing a good job for us. He was very influential, scoring a lot himself, and creating so many chances for other people. He struck up a good partnership with Robbo. I thought we had a great chance that year. We had a good squad of players and we scored goals

Alex had assembled a great squad of players. Walter Kidd, who moved into coaching with Hearts before going to Falkirk as assistant manager to Eamonn Bannon, was a real stalwart. He was a solid full-back and possessed a lot of upper body strength which he used to great effect. Over the years he had a lot of run-ins with Davie Cooper. Coop, who was never shy when it came to complaining, used to moan about the treatment he got off Walter all the time. Walter's style of running meant that his elbows played a big part and occasionally he caught Coop on the chin which he didn't like at all. Even when he moved from Rangers to Motherwell, Coop used to swear that Walter would pay to stand on the terraces and heckle him at Fir Park. But Walter was a great defender and did a superb job for Hearts over the years. The two of them had a great professional respect for each other.

Eamonn Bannon was also a good buy. He enjoyed a spell down south with Chelsea. He was a very fit guy which served him well in his wide role where he covered every inch of the touchline and delivered a lot of quality crosses.

Another follically challenged member of the Hearts side was David McCreery who also did a good job for the club. He wasn't the most technically gifted, but he was a fantastic ball winner and slotted well into the midfield.

We had a lot of good results that year. Doddy always emphasised the need for a good home record. He reckoned that if you did the business at Tynecastle and were more or less unbeatable there, you would always pick up enough points away to keep you in the league hunt. He instilled that in us and I think it's still there today. A lot of teams are scared to come to Tynecastle; it's still a tough place to get a result.

A lot has been made of the fact that Doddy never won anything, but with that little slice of luck you always need he could have won the double in 1986, the League in my first season at Hearts and gone on to even greater things.

When I arrived there was still a hangover from the bitter disappointment of losing the League and Cup in the space of a week. A few key players missed that crucial match at Dens Park through illness and Alex is still unhappy about that. To be fair to the players if you're not 100 per cent you can cost the team the match and take a hammering for not declaring yourself unfit. It's all history now, but when I first joined it was only to be expected that having been through such a shattering experience, there would still be a hangover from that.

With that Cup semi-final defeat against Celtic in 1988, we were given the unwelcome tag of bottle-merchants again. Last season we finally got through to the final and, although we lost, criticism like that doesn't really stand up. These things happen in football. If you don't concentrate for the 90 minutes you're out. People call it 'bottling', but I don't believe that for a minute. You don't play for 85 minutes as we did, having taken the lead through Brian Whittaker, and then bottle it in the last five.

Henry Smith made a mistake with two crosses at Hampden on 9 April 1988 and we were punished both times by Mark McGhee, who made a habit of scoring against Hearts, and Andy Walker. It was horrible, but these things happen to every team. Ironically when Doddy was in charge of Airdrie a few seasons later, they beat us in the semi at the same venue.

On a brighter note, even though I hated the travelling from Glasgow, I had more than a few laughs with the three other commuters – Sandy Clark, Brian Whittaker and Allan Moore. When we'd finished training we used to stock up on snacks and drink and stop off at South Gyle on the outskirts of Edinburgh to devour our lunch.

Being a footballer isn't without its perks and one of them came on a Friday when a guy called Davie, who was a big Hearts fan, used to bring in free fish for all the troops. For some reason wee Allan was the only one keen on fish on a Friday, but it was a nice gesture anyway.

One day we'd stopped at our usual spot when Brian decided to have a bit of fun and to our amusement started reversing the car back and forth like a madman; end result – some very flat fish. Allan had been laughing at Brian's antics with the rest of us, but when he discovered that it was his parcel that had tyre marks on it he was outraged.

'That's my tea for tonight,' he said, less than pleased, but Brian who was never short of a one-liner put him firmly in his 'plaice'. 'At least Kim won't have to batter it' he retorted.

Allan swore revenge and after letting things lie for a couple of weeks he scored a brilliant equaliser. A terrible smell appeared in Brian's car and after a week the whole of Tynecastle demanded he find out what it was or get rid of the car. The subsequent investigation revealed a haddock, well past its sell-by date cunningly concealed in the boot. No prizes for guessing the culprit.

On another memorable trip Brian was flashed by a BMW behind him with a guy chauffeuring two very attractive blondes in the back. Brian refused to budge and when Allan woke up in the back and found out about the road rage he promptly dropped his kit at the back window and mooned the car behind. The BMW's passengers took this well and were grinning away as they passed, but the best bit was yet to come as they pulled in front of us and the two passengers appeared topless against their rear windscreen. They kept this up while a gobsmacked Whittaker, urged on by the rest of us, tried in vain to squeeze a few more mph out of his ageing Sierra.

It was all schoolboy humour that football players excel at, but it certainly broke up a monotonous journey. When I moved back to Ibrox a few years later and was making the same trip by myself, I missed having a bit of company in the car.

Iain Ferguson was another member of the squad who liked a laugh and he came unstuck one day at a garage where we knew the general manager very well. He used to look after us when we dropped in and one afternoon we were shown into his office to wait as he hadn't returned from lunch. Fergie decided it would be a great idea to hide under his desk and crouched there for ten minutes before the door opened. When the guy sat down he shot straight back up screaming as Fergie had grabbed the most sensitive part of his anatomy.

'Got you there,' he said, with a big grin on his face which quickly changed when he realised he really had made a balls of it and scared one of the company's top men from London witless (I think that's spelled with a w).

Returning to the field of action, Alex and Sandy's approach to the game was simple. Alex was a great man for a 4–3–3 formation. Even at Ibrox he'd play with three men up front unlike some teams who regularly went there to defend, the plan being to escape with a draw and a point. Alex believed that if you attacked and scored goals, but kept it together at the back you would come out on top and we did score a lot of goals under him.

As I said earlier, Wallace Mercer always treated you with respect and tried to make you feel involved. When the time came for Alex to move on, following Sandy's departure, I was one of the first to know.

The Chairman called me in and told me 'The board has made a unanimous decision to sack Alex MacDonald. I know he's a good friend of yours, but it's happened.'

He was right, I owed Alex a lot and I've still got a lot of time for him. 'I don't necessarily agree with it, but I'll respect your decision,' I replied.

It was a devastating time for the club. Everyone had a high regard for Alex and Sandy, but the writing was on the wall when Sandy went a few months before. They were former team-mates at Ibrox and veterans of Rangers' famous Cup Winners Cup success of 1972 and the trebles of 1976 and 1978. Alex scored a memorable diving header in the Scottish Cup final, a moment that Jim Jefferies, who was in the Hearts team that day, will definitely want to forget.

Initially they had brought a new edge to Tynecastle and of course took the club agonisingly close to their first league title in decades a year before I joined. But after a great start to their management careers they hit a sticky patch the following season and we finished a disappointing sixth in the table. It seems that as co-managers, which in itself was unusual, and untried in the Scottish game, the board felt the experiment wasn't working. They were getting two conflicting decisions rather than one. They thought that a coach and manager would work better.

I thought Sandy handled it remarkably well. He said: 'I understand your decision and I'll go.' He was big enough to step aside and let Alex carry on the job alone. After that, Sandy, who was a real legend at Ibrox, stayed out of football altogether. He has carved out a new career in marketing and gone on to great things with Scottish and Newcastle Breweries, which with McEwan's Lager emblazoned on Rangers' jerseys in recent years, means he spends his Saturday's back at his old stamping ground.

Sandy's departure was a real blow to Alex, but he carried on and got the club back on the rails. Maybe when the axe fell on Alex himself his disregard for PR and courting the media was partially to blame. I've seen managers with worse records hang on to their jobs for a lot longer because the press are sympathetic, but Doddy, even though he went back a long way with a lot of the Scottish press gang, preferred to do his and his team's talking on the pitch. For a start he never used to read newspapers and given the amount of rubbish you have to read these days it was probably a wise decision.

Any trust there was between managers and pressmen has disappeared over the years and although the bosses are guilty of a few porky pies between them, some of the stories that appear are well over the top and don't help players or bosses. I'm not saying don't write bad things about teams who are losing and deserve criticism, but don't twist the facts and blow things out of proportion.

Having said that, Alex would rather be taking money off the lads playing head tennis in the gym, where he was the uncrowned champion, than taking calls about team selection, and when you had a chairman who used to milk every last ounce of publicity and was more of a media figure, it maybe didn't help.

Despite his previous record, a poor start to the 1990–91 season cost him his job and signalled the end of an era at Tynecastle.

8

ITALIA HERE I COME

The biggest thrill of my entire career was being selected for the World Cup finals in Italy in 1990. When the qualifying games kicked off I wasn't even in the international frame, so to be part of the biggest and most glamourous tournament on the planet was an unbelievable experience. I've got Andy Roxburgh and Craig Brown to thank for giving me the chance, but I was gutted over a bust-up at the end of the campaign which tarnished what had been a wonderful experience.

For all Andy and Craig achieved in their time in charge of Scotland, including qualifying for the World Cup and the European Championship in Sweden two years later, it's still a period in the Scottish game which will also be remembered for petty fall-outs and bust-ups between the management and some of the country's top stars.

And I think I'll probably go down in history as the first man to be fined a whole pound for alleged misbehaviour during Italia '90.

Every Scotland boss has come under fire for his selection policies, or the lack of them. It seems that nobody can ever pick a team or a squad and keep all of the people happy all of the time. A string of club v country rows and controversial selections have been the subject of debate among the armchair pundits and Tartan Army followers in every era.

Ally McCoist was left out of the World Cup squad for Mexico in 1986 by Alex Ferguson, and there have been others who could or should have played a part and were omitted for varying reasons. When merit and capability ceases to be part of the equation and personality clashes and petty fall-outs take their place, the fans and the country are being short-changed.

Richard Gough has become the latest star to have his portrait hung in the SFA Hall of Fame at Park Gardens, but been unable to add to the number of caps that put him there in the first place. After witnessing the bust-up that led to his international exile and then having been involved in a similarly frustrating and small-minded situation I can understand how Goughie must feel.

That unfortunate incident happened when Richard picked up a last-minute injury and Andy, who was naturally unhappy gave him some stick in a press conference at the airport before the clash with the Swiss, hinting that if he'd been injured he shouldn't have joined the squad. Richard got to hear about it and was furious, reasoning, quite rightly, that if the manager had anything to say he should have said it to his face.

Our trip to Italia '90 to play against the best teams in the world should have been a career high for me but, instead, my club partner Craig Levein and I were left with the bitterest of tastes in our mouths after another of Roxburgh's egotistical eccentricities saw all hell break loose as we crashed out of the World Cup.

In typical Scots style it was another tale of glorious failure, with some stirring performances, but the agony of just missing out on the next stage. After all that effort we were all heartbroken to be on our way home after that third match. There had been a team meeting called, solely for the purpose of thanking us for our performances and commitment. Only trouble was, Craig and I didn't realise it was compulsory. We had a few beers in the hotel bar and then headed out on the town to drown our sorrows. Despite playing well and personally feeling I had done myself proud, we had still hoped to make the final stages and were naturally upset to find ourselves packing our bags again before the tournament was over.

Short of an Argentina-like drugs scandal (allegedly), the Scottish press had a field day when Mo Johnston and Jim Bett were caught with, horror of horrors, a beer, in their hands. Pictures of them enjoying a night out in the Scots base of Rapallo were flashed back to Scotland and before we had even kicked a ball we were apologising. Maybe they should have stuck to the hotel bar and not mixed with fans, who incidentally loved every second, but there was no harm done and, having played alongside Mo and against him, I know that when the first whistle goes he's a player who gives his all for the cause. Regardless of that and the fact that they were set up by a reporter, they were condemned for breaching discipline. For their own reasons, both of them announced that they were quitting international football after the Italian campaign. What really hurt was when Andy Roxburgh shook hands with every player, including those who were in effect deserting the cause, except Craig and I. I still can't believe it was for missing a meeting when they wanted to thank us for our efforts.

When we got back the fuss didn't die down. The press got hold of it and before I knew it I got a phone call from Craig Brown.

'Dave, I think we're going to have to show that we're dealing with our disciplinary problems in the proper fashion. I think a fine, just a nominal sum like a pound, so we can say we've done it would be enough.'

I couldn't believe my ears. My reply isn't printable here, but suffice to say I never apologised or paid the fine, and just let the whole thing blow over.

Hopefully they realised they were in the wrong and that it wasn't the end of the world to miss a meeting, which was hardly vital. I'm afraid it was a clear case of the old schoolteacher mentality coming through – you're in my class and I must punish you.

They didn't treat us like grown-ups, but ultimately the whole thing was much ado about nothing. and we were both back in the frame for the qualifying games for the European Championship in Sweden. I would have been very surprised, not to mention very angry, if I hadn't been picked for the next match.

But I've never really heard Andy's side of it. As far as I'm concerned, I played three games for my country and did very well. He should have been praising us instead of slaughtering us in the press. The fact that he couldn't shake hands with us at the airport, in front of all our team-mates, is something I'll never forget. Andy did a lot for me, but you can take away a lot of good as well with those sort of gestures.

Hopefully if I ever find myself in a similar situation I'll handle it differently. I think a quiet word is always the best way to do things, but all the players knew what was going on and that was a real slap in the face.

On the plus side, the World Cup and Rapallo is an experience I'll never forget, especially as I wasn't even supposed to be there – and until the row after that final game, I was on cloud nine every time I pulled a Scotland jersey on.

To be fair to Andy and Craig, they've both done a tremendous job for Scotland and have a great record in terms of qualification for the World Cup and the European Championship. And Andy gave me all my caps, which I treasure, and he'd been a great help throughout my international career, from the World Youth Cup in Mexico, right through the Under-21 and 'B' ranks.

That trip to Mexico was fantastic, even though Mexico itself was a bit of a culture shock. Even as young pros we were used to good hotels and treatment, but the place we stayed in was more of a shanty town. The food was terrible and even though I was skinny to start with I came back even thinner.

Andy was in charge, of course, and a lot of the young hopefuls in that side ended up making it through the ranks to the full Scotland squad in years to come. We did better than anyone expected to reach the quarter-finals; being on the bench in the Azteca stadium was a fantastic experience in that atmosphere.

Nearly a decade later, my first cap against Cyprus in the World Cup qualifying campaign in 1989. was a huge honour. It was a welcome break from league duties. We met up on the Sunday and things were pretty laid back. The next day we got a lot of technical and tactical stuff from Craig and Andy. I don't think they intended it to be, but it was like school, with everything timetabled.

It might sound bigheaded, but I wasn't too surprised to be called into the squad. I had improved a lot and had gained more international experience at Under-21 level as an over age player and my name had been mentioned in the press on several occasions as being a candidate. But when the call came, it was still unexpected. I had been playing golf and called home to find that Donna's dad and my own dad had heard the news. My first reaction was 'you're joking' then I had another couple of beers to celebrate.

It was a great feeling to line up at Hampden. The match featured a classic overhead kick from Mo Johnston. I was delighted to represent my country at last and my jersey from that night still hangs in Tynecastle alongside Gary Mackay's from his Scotland debut.

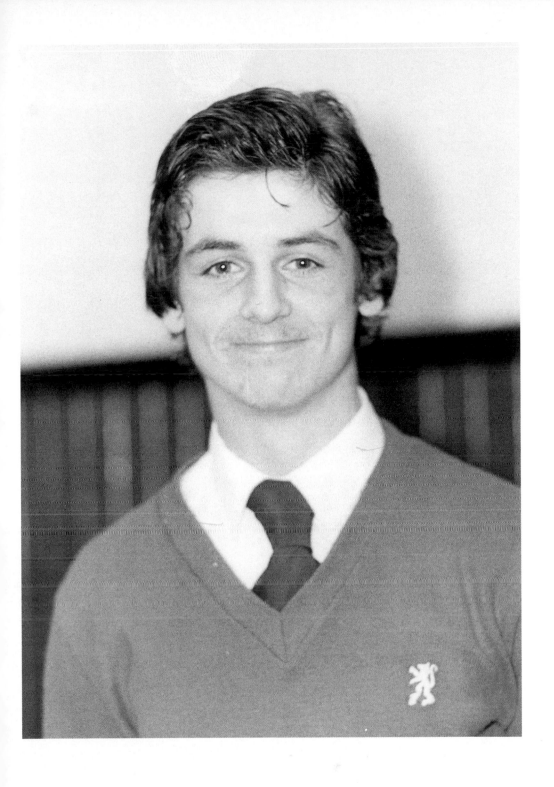

A Ranger . . . sixteen-year-old Dave McPherson after signing for Rangers in 1980.

The Rangers squad in July 1983, shortly before John Greig's departure.

The Scotland under-21 squad, with a few familiar faces, in November 1984.

ABOVE AND BELOW: Hampden Triumph: after winning the
League Cup in 1984.

LEFT: Dave grabs the Gers' first goal against Boavista at Ibrox in the 1986 UEFA Cup tie.

BELOW: Another powerful header in the 1986 UEFA Cup.

Alex MacDonald, Hugh Burns and Dave after signing for Hearts in 1987.

Derby Clash: Andy Goram and Dave do battle at Easter Road in 1987

All a Pose: Robbo and Dave at a fashion shoot.

These were exciting times. You knew if you did well you could be on your way to the World Cup, something not a lot of Scottish players, even internationalists get to do.

After the game against the Cypriots I was picked to play against England in the Rous Cup match which, again, is a fixture every player would love to take part in especially these days when such clashes with the Auld Enemy have become a rarity. On the down side we lost 2–0. Personally I knew I hadn't played well and I was disappointed with my own performance, but we had all come to the end of a long hard season and my form had dipped.

The following season the manager stated that I was now an integral part of the international set-up which gave me a real boost and I played right through to the final qualifying game.

The moment of truth came the night we faced Norway at Hampden on 15 November 1989 needing just one point to send us on our way. Coisty did the business once again, but the Norwegians equalised with a long-range effort and the final minutes of the match were unbelievably tense as another goal would have put us out of it.

In the dying seconds the ball came down the left and Jim Leighton came out early, but I managed to stop the guy with as good and as important a tackle as I'll ever make and we were on our way to It-al-eeee with the famous Tartan Army!

After the heartache of leaving Ibrox this was a total turnaround and I couldn't wait to get there. Knowing guys like Ally and Craig and a few others helped me settle into the side. For the first time in years, the majority of the squad wasn't made up of the Anglos who'd carved out a career south of the border as it had been during previous expeditions to Germany and Argentina.

Our World Cup headquarters in Rapallo were brilliant and the whole World Cup experience was just unbeatable. I've had some great moments at club level, but this is the ultimate tournament, the pinnacle of any player's career.

When we arrived we were a huge draw. Everyone was staring at us and people were looking up to us as members of one of the world's top teams.

Security was tight. We all had our pictures taken for photographic ID, with some hilarious results, and we even had our own bodyguard. One day we were taking a stroll through the town when I asked the guy what the book he carried everywhere was called. He just grinned from behind his Raybans and opened it to show us a revolver.

'Who's going to attack us?' we thought.

We got to know him well and I think he enjoyed the job as he was nearly in tears at the airport.

But as I mentioned earlier, we managed to hit the front pages as well as the back after a night off on the town. We had a couple of spare days and the management told us to get ourselves out of the hotel and have a bite to eat somewhere else. Some of the lads stayed on the seafront while others went off to watch another match in sidestreet bars and restaurants where it was quieter.

The next day, Mo and Jim Bett found themselves pictured, bottle of beer in hand and were slaughtered for supposed indiscipline. I felt really sorry for Jim Bett, who has a couple of drinks at the most and is one of the quietest, clean-living guys around. He was raging about the whole affair. They had been stitched up good and proper and made out to be real hellraisers, when they weren't doing anyone any harm and were out with permission, along with the entire squad.

Scottish international history is littered with tales of midnight excursions in rowing boats and barneys in nightclubs, but on this occasion the whole thing had been blown out of proportion.

I have to confess at this point that Craig and I did breach the rules at one point, but only to meet up with our wives. There had been a timetabled visit for the players to spend time with their families, but Donna and Carol had a nightmare journey and the delay meant we would have missed them. So we sneaked out for a couple of hours, but the most shocking thing we did was to have a shave in a local barbers while we waited for them to arrive. We enjoyed a quiet meal before heading back to camp at a decent hour.

It was great to have them there and again the whole trip was the most enjoyable I've ever had.

The European Championship is fun and a major event, but it's much smaller than the World Cup. We had already set a British record by qualifying for the finals for the fifth time on the trot and our hopes were high as we went into that opening match with Costa Rica.

It was their first appearance in the finals and at 1000/1 outsiders for once, at 50/1, we were favourites, but in front of 30,000 in the Luigi Ferraris stadium we went down 1–0 when Jaun Cayasso scored five minutes into the second half. A further blow was losing Richard Gough with a troublesome foot injury during the game. It was the worst possible start, but we knew we could still qualify if we won our remaining two matches.

And our hopes soared after just ten minutes against Sweden when I headed on a MacLeod corner and Stuart McCall grabbed his first international goal.

We knew we'd cracked it when Roy Aitken won us a penalty which Mo Johnston converted and even though we let Stromberg in for a late consolation goal, there was no stopping the memorable celebrations that night.

They don't come any tougher than Brazil, but I've never seen a team so fired up to get the win we needed in that last match. But again it was a typical Scottish story of glorious failure.

We gave it everything and at one stage big Roy had a header cleared off the line, but with eight minutes to go in the Delle Alpi stadium, Muller finished from a tight angle after Jim Leighton failed to hold a shot. Wee Mo brought a magnificent save from Taffarel at point-blank range in the dying seconds, but the scoreline stayed the same. There was still a chance that we could qualify depending on other results, but in our hearts we all knew we'd be packing our bags.

Despite the disappointment of our early exit, it was still unforgettable, particularly the last match and an experience I'll always treasure.

Off the park, as I've mentioned, things were just as enjoyable. Over the years I've known a few real characters with Rangers and Hearts, but on Scotland trips you get to meet some more players who are game for a laugh.

Now we haven't always set the heather alight in some matches, but we certainly gave a fiery performance on a trip to Switzerland even though we lost 3–1.

After the match Craig and I relaxed with a bottle of wine in our room, and it wasn't until the next morning that we realised some of our team-mates hadn't had things so quiet. The first I knew that anything was amiss was when I heard a noise in the corridor about seven in the morning. I peeped out and there was Craig Brown frantically hoovering up what we discovered later was the ash from a fire in the early hours of the morning.

We were tired after the game and even though we'd heard a few bangs during the night it didn't keep us up. It turned out there had been a dispute between some players who wanted to pay someone a visit and the unwilling occupant who had refused to open the door.

Deciding that if they weren't allowed in, the player concerned wasn't going to be allowed out, they barred the door with a pile of heavy mahogany furniture. Now, without naming names, Duncan Ferguson's a big strong guy, so pretty soon there was a furniture shop barring the door, which was fine until someone managed to set it alight. I'm led to believe that there was no real danger, but someone later produced a spoof poster based on the cover of the video for *Backdraft* which showed Ally McCoist in a fireman's uniform carrying Stuart McCall to safety.

The boys all thought that, and the actual incident, was hilarious, but the manager was less impressed, especially as we had been using the hotel in question for a number of years and they had looked after us really well. There was a reprimand for the culprit, but the incident was soon forgotten.

In another hilarious incident, in Rapallo, Alan McInally and I were locked out of the team hotel for a couple of hours.

We'd had a couple of beers to celebrate after the Sweden game and ended up on the balcony. At that point we heard a click and spotted a grinning Coisty with the key in his hand. Coisty locked us out and then proceeded to throw water on us from above and keep us out in the freezing cold. He wouldn't let us back in until we'd signed an affidavit stating that we would promise not to carry out any reprisals.

He was in top form as well during he European Championship, when we prepared for our all-important clash with Holland in unorthodox style.

We'd been given a rest day just before and Goughie, having Swedish blood, had a cousin living in Gothenburg who'd offered to show us round. We decided a quiet spot for some sunbathing was in order and found a beach outside the town. Ally and Goughie decided to go in for a swim, but I didn't fancy it as there were a lot of jellyfish and other equally unsavoury things in the water.

But I forgot my reluctance a few minutes later. As I lay quite contentedly in the sun, Ally decided to wake me up by dropping a jellyfish on my face, and I ended up charging into the water where a jellyfish fight lasted a good ten minutes.

That European Championship was another unforgettable experience and again we played some great football, even if we had nothing to show for it.

Getting a 0–0 draw with the Dutch was a great start, and from a defender's point of view keeping a clean sheet against a side that contained Marco van Basten and Ruud Gullit, was a major plus.

I'll never forget waiting for the anthem before that match and spotting Donna and Craig Levein's wife, Carol, bedecked in tartan waving like mad. Only trouble was as card-carrying members of the Tartan Army, when they came to see us after the game, the police wouldn't believe they really were players' wives and refused to let them through the barrier.

It was a real family affair with Donna's brother, Colin, and his student mates, weighed down with a tent and a huge carry-out also having a whale of a time.

Back on the pitch, we raised our game even more against Germany in the second match at Norrköping. We just couldn't stick the ball in the net and the 2–0 scoreline flattered them. We knew after that match it was all over. But we went out on another real high with a comprehensive 3–0 victory over the CIS with goals from Paul McStay, Brian McClair and Gary McAllister.

We'd battled all the way to get there and had to rely on other results after dropping points in two vital away games to Switzerland and Romania, despite fighting back to salvage a 2–2 draw against the Swiss. Oh, and it's probably worth mentioning a fluke equaliser from a Bulgarian called Nikolai Todorov, after a freak deflection off Stuart McKimmie, which took place in the same campaign, as his name was to become infamous as far as Rangers fans were concerned a few years later.

But we didn't care how we managed it. Despite our success in getting to a string of World Cups, a lot of people forget that our trip to Sweden was the first time a Scots team had managed to qualify for the European Championships.

Andy was the man behind that feat and a lot of it was down to preparation. He got the warm-up for Italy exactly right and the trip to Malta was brilliant. We trained hard, but the emphasis was on getting the squad together and making it as enjoyable as possible.

We were divided up into different groups and our squad was made up of Craig, Ally and me along with the goalies, Andy Goram and Brian Gunn. Needless to say we had a laugh a minute and downed more than a few bottles of wine.

People might say we shouldn't have been overdoing it with three of the biggest games of our lives coming up, but it helped to bond everyone together. We all got to know each other well and that was important, especially as we were going to be away for such a length of time. It made it all the more bearable.

I think that's a hallmark of all the good sides I've been in. Jock and Doddy were both brilliant at that too and when we won the treble at Ibrox in 1993 there was a happy dressing-room.

We enjoyed a trip to North America in preparation for the European Championship. Chicago was probably the highlight as far as off the field activities went.

Goughie and Dunc disappeared on their own, some of the lads went to Wrigley Field to watch the baseball while John Robertson, Gary McAllister, a few others and I went to Hancock Tower, one of the world's tallest buildings. On one of its 98 floors we had the good fortune to find the cocktail bar and restaurant where we proceeded to wash down lunch with one each of every drink listed on the menu. We then had a sweep to see who was going to pay for the meal and Gary McAllister and I lost, but as I had won the previous cut to see who was going to down the largest cocktail in the house, my name was up again, so I didn't really care about the $100 I had to shell out.

We completed a very happy day by swallowing a few more beers on the bus on the way back to the hotel. People might frown on the fact that we were enjoying ourselves, but it was all good fun, great for team spirit and vital in getting to know each other as well as possible.

I enjoyed every one of my caps with Scotland, perhaps with the exception of the last one when we crashed 5–0 to Portugal. Before the match, at Ibrox, we felt that as Rangers had done so well in the Champions League and with the importance of the back four acting as a unit, the entire Gers back four should have been picked. But Andy stuck by players he'd used before with disastrous results.

Although I've moaned about playing right-back, having been there all season with Rangers I was settled, and I wasn't overjoyed about moving back into the middle for Scotland. It's certainly my best position, but getting moved around for such a big game didn't help. We collapsed and eventually failed to qualify for the World Cup in America in 1994. It's easy to blame the manager's selection or tactics, but with a result like that the entire team has to share the blame and it simply went horrendously wrong for us on the night.

It was disappointing to finish my international career like that. I certainly hadn't reckoned on it being my last game beforehand, but I've still got a lot of great memories.

Another thing I'll always be grateful to Andy for was introducing me to Pele after our last match against Brazil in 1990. We met on the stairs on the way to an after-match press conference and spoke for a couple of minutes; but I was starstruck and didn't have a clue what to say to him. He shook hands and gave me a pat on the back and I floated back down the stairs on a real high. That's something I'll never forget. Meeting someone like that reminds you why you wanted to play football in the first place and why it's sometimes called the 'beautiful game'.

9

JOE '90

When Joe Jordan took over from Alex MacDonald at the start of the 1990–91 season, it could have been the proverbial breath of fresh air, but instead it was more like a cold front.

Going by the good relationship he had with the Scottish press when he was down south with Bristol City, he seemed to be a young go-ahead boss who recognised the value of good PR. Nothing could have been further from the truth. At times, even the players found it hard to get a word out of Joe, never mind the press gang, and it was definitely a problem for those who had to deal with him.

When he took over he was almost the complete opposite of Alex. Doddy was a bubbly character, very up front, whereas Joe had a serious personality. As a result I don't think many of the players liked him much. His best friends couldn't dispute the fact that he's a bit dour at times, but that aside, I thought he was another good boss.

He was an excellent coach and put in 100 per cent, but maybe his fatal flaw was that he wanted perfection in every game. Even the Ajax or Juventus coach doesn't get that.

If he had opened up a bit more to the press and players he would probably have lasted a bit longer. But, like Doddy, he taught me a lot and I'm grateful to him for that.

Having starred for AC Milan, the Italian influence was there for all to see. He was unjustly criticised for being defensive. In fact, he wanted to play three at the back and used two wingers most of the time. The only players with whom he talked about defence were the back four and the goalie.

The Scottish mentality still means a game of fives and a bit of a loosen up and that'll do us. But in Europe the players train morning and afternoon with the emphasis on tactics and developing ball skills.

Joe's big thing was shadow games. This means that following fitness work in the morning you spend the afternoon playing a dummy match, either against no opposition or another 11 who simply shadow you and don't tackle, intercept passes or play any active role in the match. Every player I know hates it but it's useful as you go through different scenarios that might happen on a Saturday in a training environment.

The ball would be played into a particular area after a dummy attack and Joe would step in and say, 'Right, you didn't push forward quickly enough,' or 'You're not close enough to your man.'

He worked a lot on clearing your box, which is something the Italians specialise in. When the ball comes into the area, everybody rushes out. That's something our back five practised all the time against our forwards. It worked, too.

Joe wasn't the most popular manager because he was very technical, but I liked him. He was the sort of guy you had to give a chance and get to know slowly.

Joe built a relatively successful side, one capable of pushing Rangers all the way for the title, and in 1992 we finished second in the League after a few poor results in March. But not long after that, he had a very public fall-out with Wallace Mercer. In fact, they eventually called a press conference to try to dispel the rumours of a bust-up that were sweeping the city, and present a united front.

Joe's biggest gripe was that he wasn't given the money he wanted to sign players. I think around Christmas time he had one particular deal in mind and the board wouldn't give him the cash. I think he'd been promised a lot more when they brought him in and obviously he wasn't too happy with that. I could understand Joe's point of view. We were top of the League at the time and if we had spent money then we could perhaps have done even better. In contrast every time we played Rangers that season, they seemed to have a new face. We were neck and neck with the Gers in the title race when they came to Tynecastle and more or less had to win . . . and did. It was a turning point for both clubs that season. In many ways it was the title decider.

We had bounced back from a 2–0 defeat at Ibrox in October with a 15-match unbeaten run which took us to the top of the table in January 1992. But it was downhill after that. A 4–0 gubbing at the hands of Aberdeen, our first defeat at home that season, started a slide with another shock, against Airdrie and that crucial defeat against Rangers. Coisty, who won the Golden boot that season thanks to 34 league strikes, bagged the all-important goal and virtually ended our title hopes, although we did finish a creditable second.

We also suffered another major set-back against Alex MacDonald's Diamonds when they dumped us in the semi-final of the cup. After a goalless draw we lost the replay on penalties with Scott Crabbe and I missing our spot kicks.

They sat back and hit us on the break and when it came to the final reckoning in the penalty shoot-out I missed the first one. If you look at some of the international stars who've gone through the same agony in the last World Cup finals, it gives you some comfort. But at the time it's a terrible feeling. It's worse if you're last up, miss and put your team out. Scott Crabbe was in that very unfortunate position that day and felt even worse than I did.

I would like to think there could be a better solution that's easier on players' nerves, but on other hand, it's better than the old way of settling things, by tossing a coin.

The previous season, 1990–91 we had finished an unremarkable fifth in the table, so Joe's second season was a big improvement.

That 1990 season had started badly with win bonuses a real rarity. One bright spot was the fourth league game when Robbo, Craig Levein and an own goal gave us a 3–0 victory at Easter Road, but the next result worth a mention was a hard-fought 3–2 victory at home three days before Christmas, with McPherson, Mackay and Robertson on the score sheet.

We went on to slaughter Hibs 4-1 in a satisfying victory at Easter Road and again I was fortunate to be among the goalscorers along with Tosh McKinlay, Gary Mackay and Robbo. A 5–0 thrashing from the Dons, who were certainly something of a bogey team around that period, confirmed our erratic league form. Although we did stuff Hibs again, to keep our unbeaten record against them that season, with Levein, Wright and Robertson (who else) netting, we struggled against the teams who would finish above us in the table.

Robbo was top goalscorer with just 12 league goals, with John

Colquhoun second with only seven to his credit, so it was obvious where the root of our problems lay.

To try and turn this around, Joe did manage to persuade the board to part with some cash for Ian Baird, a big powerful centre-forward, very much in Joe's mould. He had a lot of ability, but I think it's fair to say he was a bit of a nutter and got carried away at times. But Joe liked him and when he eventually moved back to Bristol he bought him again.

When Ian first arrived at Tynecastle, we were playing a game of keep ball with two players in the middle and the rest in a circle. Bairdo chased the ball and his very first tackle was straight over the top as he clattered Steve Penney.

I knew then he'd be a big hit with referees. He had a bit of a temper on him and that saw him pick up more than his fair share of yellow and red cards.

The only time Joe could be described as chatty was when you got him on to the subject of Italy; he could talk all day about that. He clearly enjoyed his time there and, because of the high standards set, like Graeme Souness, he didn't have a high regard for Scottish professionals. But they do work harder at their game than us and in general it shows.

Youngsters today are even worse than when I started when we were in morning and afternoon all the time. A lot of kids think when they've signed for a club they've made it. Actually, that's when the really hard work is just beginning.

Joe was always fairly sombre and subdued and if he was unhappy with someone's performance, say for example Robbo, he'd say 'Right, Robbo, we'll talk about it next week.' Then on the Friday he would say 'Robbo, you weren't in the box the whole game.' John, of course, would deny it and when the boss handed him a video of the game to prove his point he'd come back and happily report that he had been in the danger area four times in the first ten minutes.

John didn't let it affect him, but for other players that sort of thing the day before a game didn't really help. I always felt he'd be better getting anything he had to say off his chest on a Monday and giving you a chance to work on whatever the problem was during training that week. But Joe kept things simmering away, before letting them boil over at the wrong moment.

If he had a fault it was that he tried too hard at times. He could be really hard to handle. You'd be called into his office for something and sit there for ten minutes before he'd open his mouth.

On one pre-season trip when we were heading up north he left without five players because we were seven minutes late. Nicky Walker was driving and we got held up in the Edinburgh traffic. We couldn't believe it when we found out he'd gone. Eventually we caught the bus up to Perth where we were duly fined, which I thought was a bit harsh for something that was beyond our control.

Although I thought Joe was a good manager, he clearly wasn't happy when he got the sack and blamed what he called the 'Tynecastle Mafia', a bunch of senior pros who've been there for years, for getting him his P45. I was back at Ibrox at that point, but even from a distance I couldn't agree with his assessment.

It's often said that players get managers the sack, usually by managers themselves, but only by their performances on the field. I don't believe for a minute that board members are swayed by players' views when it comes to making that kind of decision. At a club like Hearts there is always feedback from the players and fans about how things are going, but star players demanding their gaffer gets the boot or becoming involved in a whispering campaign, are usually the ones who find themselves on their way.

But by then, I was back in blue.

10

TREBLE CHANCE

There was nobody more shocked than me to find myself heading back along the M8 to Ibrox on 4 June 1992.

It turned out to be a terrific move which left me with another five medals following treble and double-winning seasons but, to be honest, at the time I would rather have gone elsewhere.

The rumour at the time was that David Murray, another member of the Edinburgh business community, was doing Wallace Mercer, who was going through some financial difficulties following the collapse in property prices, a favour.

The move came just before I was to add to the 20 caps I had gained with Scotland in the 1992 European Championship in Sweden and I actually fancied a move down south or abroad if I was going to be leaving. There had been no shortage of rumours about other clubs' interest, but at the end of the day I had no real say.

I was surprised and not too happy to discover that Hearts had agreed a deal when they first signed me guaranteeing Rangers 25 per cent of any future transfer fee. So to get out of that and save themselves a few quid, it made more financial sense to sell me back to Rangers and make more profit on the £325,000 I had cost them first time round.

Murdo MacLeod tapped me on behalf of Borussia Dortmund and I was also involved in a bit of cloak and dagger stuff with Spanish club Seville. A guy called Jim Melrose acted as a go-between and I had a secret meeting at a Glasgow hotel with the club's president. The talks were positive and at one point he showed me a piece of paper with more zeros on it than I'd ever seen, which would have made me a peseta millionaire at least.

A couple of English clubs, Leeds and Arsenal, had shown an interest but it didn't get to the serious stage as Hearts had already agreed a deal with Rangers.

It was a move that suited the club most, although I wasn't unhappy to be going back to Ibrox. The money and the quality of the side had both improved in the years since I'd left.

All the wheeling and dealing reminded me of an earlier occasion when Southampton made a bid for me. Alex MacDonald, who was boss at the time, said: 'I've had a bid of £500,000 from Southampton, but I'm not going to sell you.'

'Thanks for telling me I said,' and headed into the club office to tell Donna the news. But as I chatted away there was a beep and a fax from Southampton rolled in so I had to hang up. This time Southampton were offering a million pounds for my signature and I was quite excited that somebody thought I was worth that much, which was a lot of cash then. But Doddy never cracked a light about it. He didn't want to sell me and he saw no use in getting me unsettled by telling me about that level of interest elsewhere.

People think players get all the inside info on the game, but in reality they're just employees and quite often they're the last to know about other clubs' interest. It was a pure fluke that I got to see that second bid from Southampton and if I didn't get to hear about that one, how many other bids did I never find out about?

And if that's happening to me, what's it like for other players?

I believe you have a right to know, but even though the players have a bit more power post-Bosman, they still don't have enough of a say in their own affairs.

The first I knew of Rangers' interest was in the run-up to the European Championship. My contract was up in June so I knew I could be leaving.

I got a call from a journalist who was straight to the point.

'Would you be interested in going back to Ibrox?' he asked.

'Of course I would,' I told him, 'but it's far too early to talk about that.'

The next step was during a Scotland trip to Norway, Walter Smith made me an offer, followed it up with a phone call and we tied a deal up really quickly. I was delighted to go back to Ibrox, especially with the way the season was to turn out. Having played alongside some of the guys who'd won Rangers' last two trebles, I knew how rare such feats were and it was great to get into the record books alongside some real Ibrox legends.

However, I was sad to leave Tynecastle. I had a good rapport with them and the club had done a lot for me. But hopefully I repaid some of that and I wanted a new challenge. I felt it was the right time to go. I've never really thought about price tags, but yes, it was nice to be a million-pound-plus rated player.

The wages and conditions at Ibrox are first class, but of course bagging a few more medals was worth even more. On Hearts end-of-season trip to Spain last season a few of us were chatting and one of the younger players asked me how many medals I had. When I told him, he couldn't believe it.

'I'd love just one of them,' he told me.

In some ways, although you try not to take things for granted, you can get a bit blasé about success. And people sometimes forget about players of the calibre of Gary Mackay, John Robertson, Craig Levein and others who don't have anything to show for all their years in the game, apart from their Scotland caps and some great memories. That kind of thing stops you getting carried away and certainly stopped me moaning about missing out on the chance of a European move because Hearts pointed me in Rangers' direction.

There haven't been too many players who've made a go of it second time round at Ibrox, so I was a bit apprehensive. Torry Gillick, Jim Baxter, Colin Stein, Willie Johnston, Derek Johnstone, Gordon Smith and Jimmy Nicholl are among those who've managed it. But a few of them failed to recapture the success they had achieved first time round.

Fortunately I went back for what was to be one of the club's most successful seasons ever. I knew I'd be leaving Hearts just before Scotland flew to Chicago to prepare for the Swedish trip. I expected to win something when I went back to a Gers side who'd just won the double, but I had no idea just how fantastic a season it would prove to be.

Winning the League at Pittodrie in 1987 was great, but clinching the fifth title in a row at Broomfield, with Gary McSwegan grabbing the all-important goal, was personally even more satisfying in my first season back with Rangers. I'd not only proved that I was good enough to come back to Ibrox but, after being sold because Graeme Souness didn't think I was up to scratch, we'd been good enough to win trophies too.

As a result I enjoyed it even more. The lap of honour at Broomfield was great. Even though there were officially just 11,830 fans there, it sounded like more. We were missing Ally McCoist who was gutted at not even being allowed to watch from the bench because of the broken leg he'd suffered playing in Portugal for Scotland. But true to form, he stole the show without even being there. A couple of fans threw on a life-sized cardboard cut-out of Golden Bollocks and he was paraded round the ground and in all the photos the next day.

All the players were tired. We just wanted to get it over with, clinching the title, and we were absolutely delighted finally to get there, especially after the disappointment of bowing out of the Champions' League with a 0–0 draw against CSKA Moscow a few days before. That was Ally's last game that season.

We had our final league fixtures before the all-important Scottish Cup final against Aberdeen a month later. I had grabbed the winner in the semi-final at Parkhead, with Coisty also on target, and I was hoping playing the final there was going to be a good omen.

Tension had been building all week, but having already beaten the Dons in the League Cup final, and beaten them 2–0 at Ibrox in March we were confident we could do it.

It was a marvellous afternoon, and even though the atmosphere at Hampden on days like that is special, playing the last ever competitive match in front of the Jungle, which was to be knocked down shortly afterwards, packed with Rangers fans, was different class.

Young Neil Murray, who'd come in and done a great job for us domestically and in Europe, grabbed one of the goals and Mark Hateley, always a player for the big occasion grabbed the other. Although the Dons pulled one back, there was never any danger that we were going to throw it away and the final whistle was the sweetest sound I've ever heard.

I'd played alongside and been managed by men like Jock Wallace, John Greig and Alex MacDonald who'd been part of the famous treble-winning teams of 1976 and 1978 and I know how much that achievement meant to them all, especially Jock who was proud of the fact that no other Rangers manager, before or since had pulled it off twice. So even though winning the League, the biggest prize, was brilliant, when we clinched the Cup at Parkhead I immediately thought of those earlier trailblazing teams and all the great players they had, especially the ones I had worked my apprenticeship under. I can't put into words just how much it meant to realise that I was part of another legendary side and we'd be up there with the greats. No one can take that away from you.

The team that day was: Goram, McCall, D. Robertson, Gough, McPherson, Brown, Murray, Ferguson, Durrant, Hateley, Huistra (Pressley), McSwegan.

When we got back to Ibrox the champagne was already flowing in the Waddell Suite. The place was packed with all the Ibrox staff, everyone from the chairman and directors to the groundsman as well as the players' wives and families.

After a while I escaped from the celebrations and decided to savour the moment to the full on my own. I grabbed an ice bucket, two bottles of champers and went up the stairs into the main stand and sat looking at the darkened ground and empty pitch. It was brilliant sitting soaking in the atmosphere. After a bit a few of the other lads who'd had a similar idea joined me. We shared the champagne and let what we'd just achieved finally sink in.

It was a fantastic season. Goughie said afterwards that the only way to top it was to win the treble again and the European Cup and he was right.

I think it's only now, after disappointments at home and in Europe that people realise just how fantastic a season that was, especially when we came so close the following year.

11

TREBLE FLOPS

After the all-time high of the previous season, there was to be more success in 1993–94 but it ended in an all-time low, with another Scottish Cup final I would never forget – this time for all the wrong reasons.

I've suffered a few setbacks in my career, but losing 1–0 to Dundee United that May afternoon was probably the worst. The biggest blow was perhaps losing out on the chance to be the only team ever to have won back-to-back trebles. On an infamous afternoon at Hampden, a defensive mix-up allowed Dundee United to snatch the only goal of the game and end their Cup jinx at last.

Afterwards I was unjustifiably slaughtered for my part in the error which led to Craig Brewster's strike. I've never really spoken about it before, but I'd like to set the record straight now.

I partly blame Ally Maxwell for all the flak I took afterwards, as he was quick to point the finger at me. I would never have done the same to him. I believe it's a team game and you share the responsibility for any defeat, even though I'll be the first to put my hand up for most mistakes.

I never like to blame other players for anything, I think it's totally unprofessional. Even when Ally Maxwell pointed the finger straight at me, which convicted me without a fair trial, I didn't get into a public slanging match with him, which would have been easy to do. If I'm going to talk about my past then that's something I feel strongly about to this day.

If you look at that goal on video, there was absolutely nothing wrong with that pass back; and even if the United player had closed Ally down quickly, all he had to do was boot the ball straight out of the park.

But that's fitba'. A year earlier I had been a hero for scoring in the semi-final against Hearts to set up the first treble. Now I was the villain after we blew our chance of making it six trophies out of six.

On the day, the team as a whole didn't perform well and even though we piled on a lot of pressure, we failed to turn it into goals and that cost us just as dearly. Without trying to criticise others, as a team we simply weren't good enough. Failing to score a goal was a rarity for us that season. Normally one goal would never have been enough to beat us.

I've now been on the losing side in three Scottish Cup finals, but I've won all four League Cup finals I've played in – them's the breaks. Even though losing in a final is hard to take, it's much better than going out in the semis

Afterwards Walter Smith exonerated me. He told me he didn't blame me and added that he thought I had been the best player in the team on the day. He might have told Maxy the same, but that was good enough for me.

I felt bad on the day but in the weeks that followed I took stick from all angles. The most sickening thing was a picture of me in a United strip on *Sun* columnist Rikki Brown's page. It was printed while I was in Canada with Scotland and was a fairly poor attempt at black humour. I'm sure a lot of people found it funny, but I wasn't laughing when I saw it on my return. I was absolutely devastated and there's no doubt that things like that reinforced the popular view that it was all my fault.

Ironically, in the first final we'd played that season, against Hibs, I *was* to blame for an own goal. For once, instead of playing in every match and then missing the final, I missed the whole League Cup campaign, but returned for the final. Early in the match I almost wished I hadn't when I scored an own goal.

Gary Stevens gave the ball away in the right-back area and a cross was played in over his head. I went for it at the near post, but it was a defender's nightmare. I couldn't leave it because I wasn't sure who was behind me, and anyway it was almost certainly going to ricochet off the post and back into the mêlée of bodies in the box.

I threw myself at it, trying to put it past the post. It looked more likely that I was going to head the woodwork rather than the ball, so I had one eye on the post. As a result, I got an ever so slight glance on it with my head which was enough to put it out of Andy Goram's reach, even though it looked as if the ball had taken a deflection off Gary Stevens.

Andy was sick at losing a goal and was cursing away, so I didn't actually own up to it until after the match. By that time we'd won the Cup thanks to an unforgettable overhead kick from Ally McCoist, which sparked yet another night of celebrations at Ibrox.

Even though I was to add another League championship winners' medal to my collection before the season was out, that year was a real non-event, marred by injuries and inconsistent performances.

For two seasons I had played non-stop football, well over 100 games including the Champions' League and the European Championship in Sweden which knackered me for the following term.

One highlight was when I battled back from injury quicker than expected to take my place in the defence for the first Old Firm clash of the season against Celtic, which I'm modest enough to think was one of my best performances. I'd missed pre-season training because of my groin problem, and that was my first match back. I was told it would take eight weeks, but I was back after five. We were missing a few other key players through injuries and for an understrength team to hold out for a goalless draw at Parkhead was a great defensive display. I couldn't walk the next day though, but at the time I reckoned it was worth it.

I had hoped that the first op would clear up the problem, but just before we faced Dundee United at Ibrox on 11 December I was told that I would have to go for another operation to correct the problem. In hindsight, which is a wonderful thing at the best of times, but especially valuable in football, I shouldn't have played. Physically and mentally I wasn't up for the match.

Sure enough, with about 15 minutes gone we found ourselves 2–0 down. Walter, who starts off in the directors' box, looked as if he'd jumped straight down to the dug-out and not bothered with the stairs. He was going absolutely mental. Shortly afterwards I put my hand up and came off injured, and ten minutes later United scored a third. I was unfortunate enough to be in the dressing-room at half time. No one was saying much, they couldn't because Watty was slaughtering everyone. Eventually he got round to me and ripped me to shreds.

'You should never have played if you weren't fit,' he bawled.

'You were definitely at fault for the second goal, and as for third . . . where the f*** were you?'

I didn't say a word. I couldn't really. But afterwards I was getting treatment when Walter strolled in.

'Slim, you weren't on the park for the third goal, were you?' he said.

'No, I wasn't,' I confirmed. 'But I felt guilty enough about the first two and you wouldn't have let me get a word in edgeways anyway,' I told him.

He apologised; though he was still upset at the result, we both saw the funny side.

Goughie came off injured during that match as well and it was definitely an afternoon to forget.

We had lots of injuries that season; a lot of people put it down to the pitch. It was a really hard surface, but once it got a bit of rain, with the grass being so short, the ball moved a lot faster on it and skidded across it.

It doesn't matter how long a stud you wear on a surface like that, it's still easy to get injured.

As I've said, after the excitement of the previous season, we all wanted another taste of the Champions' League, but a late goal in Sofia in the second-leg, qualifying match was a shattering blow. We lost 2–1 that night, but the real damage had been done at Ibrox in the first leg when we conceded two vitally important away goals at Ibrox in a 3–2 win. The following season, we were unceremoniously dumped by AEK Athens, losing 3–0 on aggregate, 2–0 to Celtic in the League and then 2–1 to Falkirk in the Coca-Cola Cup, which made August a miserable month for us.

Of course, during both those difficult spells the fans were less than delighted with the way things were going, but you come to expect that after a while. To me, it's the greatest failing of the Rangers fans that they make up their minds about some players too quickly. They don't know anything about the guy personally and before you've even kicked a ball you can be labelled as 'not being Rangers' class'. They don't realise that every player on the park goes out there and gives it their all. The fact that they're at Ibrox at all means they feel they are good enough to wear a Rangers jersey and most importantly, the manager thinks they're good enough because he picked them.

A lot of Ibrox fans are hypocritical. Peter Van Vossen is the latest in a string of stars to have borne the brunt of abuse upon arrival. Trevor Steven, Mark Hateley, Ally McCoist, Richard Gough and even Duncan Ferguson and Paul Gascoigne have all been targets over the years, but every one of them has proved the punters wrong. Mark wasn't fit when he arrived at Ibrox and neither were Gazza nor Van Vossen, who now looks a totally different player from the one Walter bought the previous season.

What I found difficult to handle was that I was taking a lot of stick when I was playing out of position, even during 1992–93 when I played in almost every game in every competition and we cleaned up. You hope that the fans are educated in football terms and understand that even if you are giving it your best shot at right-back, you're always going to produce a better performance at centre-half where you feel most comfortable, and you're never going to be as good in a different role.

You can understand them being critical of the team if it isn't performing, but it could be a bit more constructive. I never said it at the time, but they could certainly have been a bit more supportive. All that having abuse hurled at you does is destroy confidence and make players afraid to try anything. Then the harder they try to get the fans off their back the more their concentration goes and the worse their performance is.

The most hurtful things are the sarcastic remarks, which you can hear on the park no matter how big the crowd is. They really get to you. At times I've felt like running into the stand, handing them a jersey and telling them to go on and see if they can do better. They feel they've paid their money and they have the right to shout abuse.

As I've said, I wasn't alone. Some people will argue that if you take the applause you have to take the down side too, but some of it really is unjustifiable. Ian Ferguson is another example. Fergie is an outstanding player, but because his career has been disrupted by injuries, especially in his early days at Ibrox, even though he's one of the biggest bluenoses in the dressing-room, he's never been loved or appreciated by the fans in the way Graeme Souness and Walter Smith, who both stuck by him, appreciated his talents.

With every championship Rangers win, the supporters get more blasé about the whole thing. Rangers winning their eighth title on the trot last season was a magnificent achievement; but if they fail in their bid to equal Celtic's record of nine on the trot, they'll probably be regarded as failures! It's ridiculous – two or three is a fantastic achievement. At Tynecastle we'd probably settle for just one.

We won the League that season at Easter Road, even though we lost to Hibs. Compared to previous title parties, the atmosphere was flat, simply because of the Gers fans reaction to defeat, even if they have won the League.

You have to put it in context. A decade before we wouldn't have cared if we'd lost 6–0 to Hibs, as long as the championship-winning flag was going to be flying above Ibrox the following season.

Once we were on the coach heading back to Glasgow and stopped off at the Royal Scot Hotel on the outskirts of Edinburgh for a few beers we started to celebrate and it finally sunk in that despite all our problems that season we'd won the title again, even though we had lost on the night.

I can't emphasise enough that it's what you do over the course of the season that counts, not just one match. I'm sure Hibs would gladly have swapped places with us.

I missed the following match, another defeat for an understrength team at Kilmarnock, but I was back in the side for the six-in-a-row party in the final league match against Dundee at Ibrox where the champagne flowed once again after the teams had played out a goalless draw.

It wasn't the most convincing run-in. We hadn't won a match in a month and ironically the last victory was 2–1 against United at Ibrox, followed by a defeat against Motherwell, a draw with Celtic and those defeats against Hibs and Killie.

That victory at Tannadice was also Andy Goram's tenth and final appearance that season. Our injury jinx meant he didn't kick, or catch, a ball for us until the following February. Losing him in the run-in to the League and, worse, the Cup final had a huge impact. Also struggling were Stuart McCall and John Brown, who missed the final, and throughout the season Goughie had a few problems as well. Ally McCoist only started 19 times, plus nine off the bench, and scored just 11 goals. Big Mark Hateley, who set up as many as he scored in their successful partnership, responded magnificently with 30 goals from 52 appearances.

It's easy to forget that we actually won two trophies that season, but it's still one of the least memorable on record. And for big Duncan Ferguson, who arrived at the start of the season for a shortlived British transfer record fee of £4 millon, it was even worse. Fergie is destined to be one of the greatest Scottish strikers ever, but he came to Rangers at the wrong time and it just didn't work out for him.

He was desperate to do well for Rangers, but in the end he only scored once that season, against Raith Rovers on 16 April as we handed out a 4–0 gubbing. It's a match he'll remember for all the wrong reasons after the infamous head-butting incident with Jock McStay which cost him a red card, a ban and, eventually, his freedom.

I was on the pitch when they squared up and went head to head, and I still don't think Dunc touched him. He maintains to this day, even after his prison sentence, that he was innocent. Players do get involved in the heat of the moment, but there have been worse cases before and since, and to my mind Fergie was made a scapegoat. I firmly believe that discipline is the SFA's job and even if he was guilty, Fergie would have been punished severely enough by them without the police becoming involved. Where else in Scotland can you be fined thousands of pounds and jailed for the same offence?

What was really sickening was the Junior Cup final a few weeks later which produced a performance that Frank Bruno would have been proud of with a huge punch-up. Was there any police action taken? No danger. On that occasion the law was definitely an ass.

Of course, part of Duncan's problem was a bit of previous during nights out. I wasn't present so I can't comment on those, but every Rangers or Celtic player knows the problems you can get from rival fans or people who are jealous of your success and the hassles that causes.

Duncan, to me, was just a big, honest guy who loved the game, loved playing for Rangers and loved a laugh. Before he joined us he would always chirp away at you on the park. On one occasion when he was playing for United, he sidled up to me and said, 'I think I'll come over here and win a few headers, I'm sick of beating Goughie in the air.'

After he'd won one out of ten against me, he said, 'See you later big man, I'm away to see Goughie now.'

He was always very confident as well as talented and he's finally showing what he can really do with Everton. I hope he's a huge success there and with Scotland.

Just before I rejoined Hearts there was another famous punch-up, this time between Craig Levein and Graeme Hogg in August 1995 at Stark's Park. When I went back to Tynecastle, Craig told me about it. Hoggy was a nice, big guy but he could get on your nerves on the park, he would just do his own thing. Pre-season games tend to be a bit frantic when you're trying to get your shape and get organised for the coming campaign. Craig was shouting out instructions to mark and pick-up and Graeme just blanked him completely. Eventually he said something back to Craig, they both squared up, Craig lost his temper and delivered a crisp uppercut. Hoggy was stretchered off and both of them were red-carded.

Now there's no way you do that and the club lets you get away with it; you are punished and if it had been handled internally it would all have blown over quicker. Craig had already been stripped of the captaincy, and was then hit with a ten-match ban by the SFA, something which didn't help the club that season at all.

Craig was understandably less than chuffed with Raith Rovers who were videoing the game for training purposes, and let it be used by the TV companies, which made matters a lot worse.

It's hardly a good advert for the game and Craig would be the first to admit that he was in the wrong, but these things do happen in football, I don't know how many times a season. The problem is that once an incident is shown on television, it's repeated again and again. They'll tell you that they have a duty to their viewers to show these things, and that it's up to the players to set an example. But while I would never like anything covered up, I think TV companies should set an example as well and not show these things again and again.

My son Christopher is football-daft. When he's not wearing a Hearts strip he's running around being Cantona, which is fair enough until he decides he's going to be Eric's 'dark side' as seen on TV, and starts shoving people around. If he'd asked me why Cantona wasn't playing after that infamous Crystal Palace incident, I would simply have told him that he'd been sent off for being bad and left it at that.

He's at the sort of age when I'm thinking of seeing if Coisty can get him on *Question of Sport* because he eats and sleeps football and soaks up every detail and has probably watched my Hearts videos more than I have. You know you're in real trouble when he wakes you up to tell you that some Vauxhall Conference League side have sacked their manager.

So when he sees things like that shown time and time again it sets a really bad example. I'm not condoning either players' actions, but I do think it glamorises the ugly side of the game, and I'm not talking about Craig's face here. Going back to Duncan, I don't think he was in the right either, but the television footage made the whole incident seem a lot worse than it actually was.

Another big money transfer which didn't work out was the capture of French international defender Basile Boli. I always thought Basile was a good player. Just recently his name came up in conversation with Gilles Rousset who told me that, until Basile got a bad injury in France, when he was younger he was absolutely outstanding – no one got past him. That was certainly the impression I got from playing against him and then watching him in action for Marseille against AC Milan in the European Cup final. So like everyone else I was disappointed when he arrived at Ibrox and just wasn't the player everyone expected him to be.

He was heavily criticised for remarks he was supposed to have made about his team mates. He fell foul of Walter for failing to adhere to the strict Ibrox dress code which demands a collar and tie in all but exceptional circumstances. The gaffer let him off a couple of times because he was new to the club, but finally lost patience and sent him home to change. After that I think his days were numbered.

He wasn't the only one. Rumours started to circulate about Alan McLaren moving from Hearts and me moving in the opposite direction. Walter told me on a number of occasions that this wasn't the case, but eventually the predictions came true.

He called me into the office and said he'd put in a bid for Alan McLaren and Hearts wanted me back in return. I asked him what my future would be at Rangers and he told me simply, 'You're not part of my long-term plans.'

I said that I'd go and talk to Hearts and if I could agree terms then I wouldn't mess about. He wasn't best pleased when I returned to

Ibrox after some informal talks, where terms weren't even mentioned.

He called me back into the office and wanted to know why I wasn't going, but I told him again that I'd go when I'd agreed terms and I wasn't rushing into anything. I asked if I didn't go to Hearts was I still up for sale. 'Not necessarily' was the answer, but finally he said that I'd be allowed to go for £750,000.

'I'm not staying at a club who doesn't want me,' I told him and went back to Hearts. After further discussions I agreed terms with them.

I was disappointed at the time, especially as I'd been part of a side that had won five out of six domestic trophies in my first two seasons back. But deep down I didn't think things had been right since that disastrous Cup final defeat. I've known Alan McLaren for a lot of years at Tynecastle and he stays close to me in Edinburgh. I was genuinely happy for him to get a big move.

Off the park Alan is extremely quiet and at first I thought that might be something which would hold back his career. But he's entirely different the moment he crosses the touchline and I think the turning point for him was doing a great job of man marking when he made the international breakthrough. He followed Roberto Baggio all round Ibrox one evening in a friendly against Italy and, believe me, marking a huge star like that out of a game looks great on anyone's CV.

After I left Ibrox I found myself back there on 1 May 1995. One of the saddest moments of the season was the shattering news that Scott Nisbet was being forced to chuck it through injury, aged 25. Football can be a cruel game and just three days after his wonder goal against Brugge in the Champions' League, Nissy played his last competitive game in a Rangers jersey, a 2–1 defeat at Parkhead. His career was tragically cut short on the diagnosis of a serious pelvic problem which could have crippled him if he'd carried on.

Nearly 30,000 turned out the following season to pay tribute to him in a Rangers v Rangers International Select side which brought back a few familiar faces to the club. Highlight of the evening was sharing the dug-out with Graeme Souness and a cardboard cut-out of Ally with a bubble coming out of his mouth saying 'Aw naw, not again', a cheeky reference to the time 'The Judge' spent on the bench under our old gaffer. Times have changed and even Graeme saw the funny side.

It was good to line up with my old drinking buddies Terry Butcher and Chris Woods again in the select side which also included old Ibrox favourites like Derek Ferguson, Mo Johnston, Graham Roberts, Kevin Drinkell and Ray Wilkins.

Nissy arrived at Ibrox just a few years after me and despite his youth he had a lot of first-team experience. Like me, a lot of people didn't think he would make it, but he constantly confounded the critics, especially Souness. Even being thrown a league handbook and told to pick himself a club didn't phase Nissy. He stayed to fight for his place and was a great servant to the club.

Like myself, Nissy took more than his fair share of stick from the Ibrox boo-boys, but a lot of it was good-natured. When he set off on one of his mazy runs, the whole stadium was on its feet waiting to see what he would do next.

12

EUR UNBELIEVABLE

I've enjoyed some magical nights in Europe over more than a decade, but the closest I've ever come to a medal was the season Rangers made their debut in the inaugural Champions' League – without doubt *the* top club competition in the world.

We were agonisingly close to the ultimate clash and I still believe if we had got to the European Cup final against AC Milan, we would have beaten them to become real Ibrox legends. I'm really proud to have played in every game in our tremendous ten-game unbeaten run that season, one of only three players to do so.

At the time I don't think anybody, especially the fans, understood just how big an achievement it was to be one win away from the European Cup final. The failure of Rangers and other Scottish clubs to make their mark again at that level underlines just how tough it is to get close to what is the ultimate prize for any club.

We didn't know what we were letting ourselves in for when we kicked off the campaign. Rangers' and other Scottish clubs' traditional role of glorious losers, usually just one frustrating goal away from the following round, was still fresh in the memory when we took on Danish champs, Lynghby.

It was my first game back in Europe with Rangers and I have to admit it wasn't the best of starts. I didn't have a good game, made a few passes that could best be described as interesting and took a bit of stick from the Gers fans. You learn to expect that at Ibrox where the crowd are never slow to let you know when you go wrong. It wasn't a great team performance and the Danes, who included Morten

Weighorst who's now with Celtic in their ranks, weren't a bad side.

I think a lot of supporters and the press half expected us to go out in that round, but we got it together for the second leg in the Parken Stadium in Copenhagen and I'm glad to report that, having taken over for the injured Richard Gough in my favoured centre-half role, I made amends for my dodgy start.

Rangers vice chairman, Donald Findlay, told me afterwards that he thought I was the best player on the park which was nice. Every player needs a pat on the back at the right time and it helped my confidence in the league campaign. I was back in the more familiar right-back spot for our next big test against Leeds United.

Those two ties were ones which nobody involved in them, in the crowd or watching on TV, will ever forget. The build-up for what was immediately dubbed the Battle of Britain was unbelievable. There was so much pressure on the players but nobody wanted to win the two games more than them and I think that showed. We were supremely confident. No one in our camp even thought about losing. You can be overconfident at times and it can work against you, but we were simply determined to go through. And the team spirit and battling qualities saw us through.

We weren't quite as cocky when Gary McAllister blasted Leeds ahead as some fans were still taking their seats, and Ibrox fell silent. The atmosphere in the stadium for European ties is always electric and the noise during the warm-up and at kick-off had been frightening. After that initial shock, both the fans and players recovered and they roared us on as we dug deep for a famous win.

I had a hand in Ally's second goal, and managed to get injured in the process when a Leeds defender flattened me as I flicked the ball on.

Thanks to Leeds' keeper John Lukic we were 2-1 up at the interval and in the second half the big danger was that we had put that much into salvaging things in the first 45 minutes, there was nothing left in the tank. Leeds were the better team for a spell, but we finished on top which was a nice bonus going into the all-important second leg.

Leeds, having scored an away goal were still confident and thought they would swagger to an easy win when they got us on home turf. They didn't realise that we didn't think we could lose it. Gary

McAllister, who obviously had to produce his own propaganda, predicted the opposite.

He told me: 'We've got the home support, we're unbeaten at Elland Road and we're playing Glasgow Rangers.'

As the history books show, he was wrong. Big style. Mark Hateley, Ally McCoist and Ian Durrant, who scored and crafted our two goals, got the credit they were due, but the whole team worked their socks off.

Dale Gordon, who had joined us from Norwich City, played right midfield in front of me that night and put in a power of work. He had an absolutely tremendous game and even though he was better known for his attacking skills, he tackled like a madman and had a great game, covering for me if I pushed forward.

Our 4–4–2 solidity was very hard to break down and Andy Goram made a crucial stop from Eric Cantona with just a few minutes on the clock which had a few nerves jangling.

But when we pulled back the away goal so early in the game, we knew it was going to be our night.

Mark's not well-known for his long-distance goals, but his strike was a classic. You could tell he was going to shoot when the ball dropped invitingly for him, but I don't think Lukic had a clue. He should have had it covered from that range, but the ball scorched past him into the net.

Having been left out of the English international set-up, it was a great moment for Mark. The second goal meant everything to Ally McCoist who had a lot to prove that night as well. Not to his team-mates, or any of the Ibrox diehards who were on an undercover mission in an audience that was supposed to be made up entirely of Leeds fans. He'd played in a less than successful Sunderland side and a lot of English fans had written him off as not being a great striker and one who couldn't find the net in the First Division. But Ally was at the very top of his game. He was in absolutely lethal form for the entire season and I think that goal, a diving header even, delighted him. The movement off the ball, the cross from Mark after a great pass from Ian Durrant and a clinical finish made it one of the best goals I've ever seen and Ally's normal well-rehearsed, crowd-pleasing celebrations were forgotten as he sunk to his knees before being mobbed by blue jerseys.

Leeds pulled one back, but the game was all but over after that second goal. As we came down the tunnel the United players were broken men. They just could not believe they'd lost at home . . . and to a Scottish side! Meanwhile we were singing, dancing and hugging each other as the celebrations, which lasted well into the wee small hours started.

It was crazy stuff on the team bus from Elland Road back to our hotel in Manchester. Even the normally serious Oleg Kuznetsov had a grin on his face as he and Alexei Mikhailichenko got stuck into the beer in the back seat. The only player not smiling was Pieter Huistra, who was a victim of the three-foreigner rule and had made way for Dale. He was gutted not to be a part of it, but the rest of us were on cloud nine or higher.

The mobile phones were red-hot as the troops phoned home to let friends and family sample the party atmosphere. But, typically, as I tried to call Donna and Christopher to let them know I was okay my phone went on the blink. All the jumping up and down and singing on the bus turned it into a sauna which had wreaked havoc with the electrics.

The celebrations were well into extra-time before we called it a day. We caught the first flight back to Glasgow and prepared for the more pressing business of winning the League.

It was a fantastic feeling, but gradually we realised that we hadn't actually won anything and we prepared for the final stages of the Champions' League, matches which we all knew would be even tougher.

But having qualified, the pressure was off us and I don't think anyone expected that we would go so close to making the final and not lose a game.

The new league set-up meant that rather than living in terror of losing a goal at home you could be more attack-minded. If you lost one, then you just had to score more. This theory was well tested in our first clash against Marseille. Normally losing two goals at home to a side of that calibre would have been suicidal, but on the night an opportunist header from Mark Hateley, a fine performance from supersub Ian Durrant which virtually turned the game and a late equaliser from Gary McSwegan, a goal he'll never forget, salvaged a point.

Tragically, Derek Ferguson's baby daughter Lauren died that night and our thoughts turned to the Ferguson family.

Marseille and the other teams we faced all had top quality players, but what we had was a team spirit and determination which was unmatched and that gave us the edge in every game. We were on £20,000 a man to qualify for the final stages by beating Leeds and £3,000 per point after that. But although the money was a great bonus, when you're out there on the pitch that doesn't come into it. You're playing for your own pride and the team's. We earned a lot of money that season, but compared to the cash the club was making, somewhere in the region of £220,000 per point, plus various commercial spin-offs, it was nothing.

If the players loved the competition, then the fans were just as happy and looked forward to more than a few beers and the chance of getting away. We enjoyed great support home and away and the majority of the fans were really well behaved. They respect the countries they go to and the people they meet. Of course, there's always the minority who will misbehave no matter where they are, and if you go in and noise them up you'll definitely create trouble and probably get more than you bargained for in return.

Everything built up nicely. Throughout the season we had a very settled side which helped and we were more than ready for the return trip to Marseille, one of the biggest games everyone at the club had been involved in. A win over there would have all but qualified us for the final, and even the 1–1 draw thanks to a superb strike from Ian Durrant meant we were still in with a chance going into the final game with CSKA Moscow at Ibrox.

There was a lot of hype beforehand, but it was a great experience for everyone involved. The club organised things well, laying on a plane for the players' wives, which was a nice touch. On the way back, they were on a plane full of supporters and at one point they thought they had hit a lot of turbulence, but it was simply the punters singing and dancing up the back. The plane was literally jumping.

Before the game I spotted a large police presence round a less than sober group of girls, who turned out to be our own wives. Not only were they flying with the bears, they had started to act like them as well. Sitting three rows behind them, sober, I spotted my brother Jim who had travelled all the way from London by train for the match.

We always go for a snooze in the afternoon before a match, but for once I didn't sleep that well which showed just how big an occasion it was. We went for a stroll to stretch our legs and down the hill from our hotel, which overlooked the sea, we spotted the French Foreign Legion recruitment base. The joke was that if we didn't win we'd be back to sign on for a few years.

The Velodrome was a strangely shaped stadium, and even though we could hear thousands of the Light Blue brigade going mental behind the goal, it wasn't the best atmosphere I've played in.

The game itself was nothing special and both sides played it very cagey. I think they would have settled for a draw, but we were desperate to win. After we lost an early goal it was a great relief when Ian Durrant hit a rising volley into the corner of the net. It was one of the best goals Durranty's ever scored, and he's scored a few.

The bit he enjoyed the most though was being able to ask Coisty on numerous occasions 'How many Champions' League goals have you scored then?' Ally's since had his revenge with a super strike for Scotland in the European Championship in England, plus his remarkable hat-trick to confirm his standing as Rangers' all-time European predator.

Having kept our unbeaten run going, we were still in with a shout. Everything rested on that final game against the Russians, which was the hardest game by far, and on events in Belgium where Marseille's fate was still in their own hands.

We harboured slender hopes of realising our elusive Euro dream, but they faded away in the cauldron of Ibrox that soon turned into a real vale of tears. We could tell from the crowd that they were more or less through, and as the game wore on it became clear that no matter what we did, nothing could stop them from reaching the final. That was the most heartbreaking thing and the hardest to swallow. We finished the tournament unbeaten and still had nothing to show for all our hard work.

It was all a huge anti-climax. Everyone was crying in the dressing-room in what was a very emotional night for the players and fans. We carried our luck, every team does, but to be so near and not get to the final left us all gutted. We got a standing ovation from the crowd which was the only high point of a very frustrating evening and left around 45,000 people with lumps in their throats.

We hadn't won enough games. It was as simple as that, but there was a depressing footnote to the whole business. When we played in Marseille, the club took the precaution of doing their own catering, having flown chefs, waiters and supplies in from Glasgow, presumably because it had been rumoured that the French would stop at nothing to try to gain a victory, off or on the field. It's the kind of thing that undoubtedly does go on abroad and Marseille were said to have pulled a similar stunt when another French club arrived on league business. This was never proved, but I think our precautions were vindicated when umpteen Marseille directors and officials, including the club's flamboyant owner Bernard Tapie, were found guilty after an investigation into a bribes scandal and Marseille were stripped of the European Cup.

There was some suggestion that the final should be replayed with ourselves and AC Milan, but I always thought that was a non-starter. There's no doubt they were up to no good, but as far as I'm concerned the better team went through. They proved that in the final when they stunned Milan with their poised performance and I doubt very much if they would have been able to influence Milan, with millions of pounds up for grabs for the winners.

It would have been brilliant for us to have got to the final, but not that way. If we had, I believe we would have won it. The way the season was going with a squad of players who would have killed for their team-mates and were so comfortable with each other off and on the park, I really don't think we could have lost it.

That whole experience was light years away from my European debut in the Cup-Winners' Cup of 1983–84 when I grabbed four goals in an 8–0 demolition job on Maltese part-timers Valletta.

It was the perfect start and since then I've had a great record in Europe and some memorable nights with Rangers and Hearts.

I had never been abroad until I joined Rangers. Then at just 16 I found myself off to Canada and spent three weeks living out of a suitcase, followed by a world tour to Australia which lasted four or five weeks.

Some of the older players were complaining about the length of time they were away, but although I didn't have to worry about a family, there was no way I was going to join in. I knew how lucky I was to be there, staying in the best hotels with all expenses paid. There was a lot of flying and hard travelling as well, but you just have to decide that you're going to enjoy it.

When I first started, you didn't have the luxury of direct flights from Glasgow to even the most accessible of European countries. London was the first stop on what was usually a five-day trip. Nowadays it's like an SAS mission. Straight in, do the job and out as fast as you can, leaving on a Tuesday and returning on the Wednesday night.

With average flight times of around two and a half to three hours, if a European league is ever set up team buses will be a thing of the past. It'll simply mean flying in for the game and home again afterwards, probably a more comfortable journey than Pittodrie is now.

Although it all sounds great fun, believe it or not there is a down side to all this. Boredom is still a major factor. Unlike most tourists, you're not free to go as you please and endless hours spent in hotels, particularly without a drink, can drive you up the wall. It's normally sleep, eat, train, play. The walkman is the greatest thing since someone chopped up a loaf as far as players are concerned. Portable computer games and being able to take your own videos with you cut down on the endless hours of no entertainment and save you losing a fortune in the card schools which a lot of players enjoy.

But even though I've loved staying at some of the world's top hotels, I've also been in some of the most cockroach-infested dives Eastern Europe has to offer. I still shiver at the memory of the Scotland team's chef, who was borrowed from a Glasgow nightclub for the match, disgustedly showing me around the kitchen he was supposed to prepare food in. It would have made your flesh crawl, just like the other occupants of the room did.

Then there was the ill-fated Mostar mission with Hearts a few years back. We had to charter a plane to Split which if you know your former Yugoslavian geography, is on the coast, while Mostar is right in the middle of the country surrounded by mountains. Even Biggles couldn't get a charter plane in there, so we faced a long flight and then an even longer coach journey. Full-scale war hadn't yet broken out, but there were still enough burnt-out army lorries along the way to make us more than a little nervous.

Of course, there are more enjoyable places to visit, like Malta where you can top up the tan. Those two games against Valletta in 1984, which finished an incredible 18–0 on aggregate and a home tie against Oporto were my first and last under John Greig who resigned before the away leg in Portugal on 18 October 1983, with Tommy McLean taking over the hotseat for a brief period. We played well over there but a 1–0 defeat and the away goals rule after a 2–1 home win saw us make an early exit.

Europe is the best place to learn more about the game. Even before those matches, my very first taste of it was in my early days at Ibrox when Rangers were drubbed 5–0 by Cologne. I was part of the squad, and even though I wasn't a sub, I watched bemused as the Germans and Pierre Littbarski in particular, ran riot. It was a real education to see the quality crosses the Germans were firing into the box. They really were different class, but I'm sure my team-mates weren't quite as interested in the finer points of the games as I was.

The following season, 1984–85 was the traditional one of glorious failure and two of the most memorable foreign experiences I've ever had.

We drew Inter Milan in the second round of the UEFA Cup and the atmosphere in front of 65,000 fans in the San Siro was unbelievable. We lost 3–0 with Ian Redford smacking the bar with a tremendous volley which might have set up a famous victory.

This was also the time of Big Jock's famous tactical switches when he decided that skipper and centre-half John McClelland was the ideal candidate to 'rumble 'em up'.

In those pre-video days and before the explosion of foreign soccer coverage on satellite television, your first look at the opposition was usually in the warm-up; or it was like *Mission Impossible* – 'Here is the man you will be marking. This photograph will self-destruct in five seconds.'

I had learned a lot from the first leg and we played a lot better when we got them at home. Iain Ferguson, who was to score one of the best goals I've ever seen for Hearts against Bayern Munich, found the net twice as we romped into a 3–1 lead. But with players of the quality of Walter Zenga, Franco Baresi and Liam Brady in their ranks, they held out to go through on the away goals rule.

The previous round was just as nerve-racking, but for all the wrong reasons. We lost 3–2 to Bohemians in Dublin with Coisty and yours truly getting our goals, but even the San Siro had nothing on the 10,000 crowd in Dublin that night.

There was absolute mayhem with a rematch of the Battle of the Boyne on the terraces despite Big Jock out on the pitch trying to calm things down. There were a lot of arrests and even more injuries and it didn't stop there as supporters' buses were stoned and bricked on the return journey.

It was a terrible time. A lot of Rangers fans had come down from Belfast and Ulster and the religious divide was the widest I've ever seen it. It was sheer hatred. Any time a Rangers player went near the touchline there was a barrage of bottles, bricks and even darts, with nobody doing anything to stop it. I felt sorriest for Nicky Walker who was a sitting target and couldn't go near his goal-line otherwise he was going to be catching more than the ball.

Unbelievably, the next morning in the papers we took stick for the number of goals we had lost. I thought this was so unjust. Playing in that environment, it was impossible to concentrate, with the Gardai attacking the Rangers fans and vice-versa and we were frightened it would spill on to the park. Big Jock was a man who was scared of nothing and he taught his players to be the same, but inside I think we all were, and rightly so.

It's fair to say that it wasn't my most enjoyable trip.

The Ibrox leg of the tie was a disaster for 84 minutes and it looked as if we were out until Craig Paterson and Ian Redford grabbed two late goals.

I don't know why the violence was so bad. I've played there with Hearts when we faced St Patrick's Athletic in the UEFA Cup in 1988 and the fans mixed happily and enjoyed more than a few pints of Liffey water together. We've just returned from a pre-season trip there and despite the flare up in violence, we had no problems whatsoever.

Around that time, apart from Aussie winger Dave Mitchell, and the odd Irish player, the squad still had a real tartan flavour to it and even though we weren't meeting with the same success as past Rangers sides, there was the odd flashback to old glories.

It made you take your hat off to the '72 Cup Winners Cup team; it was an even bigger achievement to win with an all-Scots side, and with the restriction on foreign players being binned and the barriers coming down, it doesn't matter if a team's from Italy, France or wherever, it's going to be rare to see a team made up of just one nationality picking up any silverware.

Jock played a big role in that famous victory, but the season after that Dublin débâcle, 1985–86 turned out to be his last in European competition. We had an ever shorter stay in the UEFA Cup, being dumped by Atletico Osasuna 2–0 after a 1–0 home win with Craig Paterson heading the winner once again. It was a bitter blow and hardly the farewell Jock would have wanted, had he known he would be on his way.

When Graeme Souness took over the reins we all had high hopes and got off to a good start with a 4–0 home win over Ilves Tampere of Finland, with Robert Fleck grabbing a hat-trick. But the gaffer was less chuffed when we lost 2–0 over there.

I've got happier memories of the next round, though, as the old McCoist–McPherson scoring partnership gave us a 2–1 win over Boavista and Derek Ferguson fired us into the next round with a 1–0 away win.

The next step, in November and December of 1986, was to be my last in a Rangers jersey until the inaugural Champions' League season in 1992.

And I certainly went out with a bang as Davie Cooper and Stuart Munro were both ordered off for retaliation against Borussia Monchengladbach. That match summed up all that's bad about European competition and the cynical tactics of some of the teams.

A 1–1 draw at Ibrox meant that the away goals rule after a goalless draw over there, was enough for the Germans. It was a real kicking match against Borussia Moenchengladbach and the referee lost the plot early on. The Germans knew exactly how to wind us up and we fell into the trap. Coop and Stuart could hardly be described as dirty players but eventually couldn't take any more and were red-carded for retaliation.

My other continental capers with the Gers were two fun-filled trips to Athens and Sofia, trips that everyone involved in will want to forget. Still flushed with our initial assaults in the qualifying round for the Champions' League, and victims of a questionable seeding process, we faced a preliminary round tie against AEK Athens which was a real disaster.

Then, of course, there was the ultimate sickener against Levski

Sofia when a freak goal seconds from the final whistle saw us humiliated again as we crashed out before we'd fired a shot in anger against the big guns. We were on £25,000 a man to qualify that night and we watched Nikolai Toderov's speculative 50-yard shot fly past Ally Maxwell in total disbelief.

Being honest we lost that tie at home by being extremely naïve and Scottish, for want of a better description. We were 2–0 up, lost a goal, scored another and let them cling to the lifeline of not just one but two away goals. We were cruising at 2–0 and we should have settled for that, but we were overconfident and went chasing more goals to make sure. Any self-respecting European team would have sat tight, and if there's one thing we're always confident of it is scoring goals away from home.

We didn't carry any luck in Sofia and Athens just came too soon for us. They weren't a great side, but they weren't bad either and obviously I reckon Walter Smith made a big mistake in the team selection because he didn't play me, opting to use Gary Stevens, a right-back if ever there was one, as a left-sided centre-half.

Earlier, we had played a pre-season game against Kaiserslautern and lost – but to us it was just pre-season, the result wasn't the most important thing and nothing worth worrying about.

But before we played in Athens the boss pulled me aside and told me 'I'm not playing you because I don't think you look sharp enough for the game.'

'What games are we talking about, in pre-season?' I asked. 'I will be sharp enough.'

'Sorry, I've made the decision.'

'Fine, but I don't agree with you,' I told him and left it at that.

Even if he had dropped me, I thought he should have gone for reliable players with experience in their own position and not use someone who'd hardly ever been involved in such a role. Then, if they don't have a good game they'll take the blame. But to be fair to Walter the team didn't play well that night; we just didn't play as a team or help each other out, the things that had been our main strengths in 1992–93. We couldn't salvage things in the second leg and were shown the door again.

But all these games I've talked about have been part of a great learning process. I don't think there's any doubt that Walter Smith will build a great team for Europe, although he had a great one when I was in it!

Apart from the season when Juventus stood head and shoulders above everyone else, the most difficult matches are at the qualifying stages. They always throw up tricky teams and come far too early in the season for any Scottish side. But in the early stages of the Champions' League where away goals aren't punished so heavily, anything can and probably will happen.

It's great to be with Hearts back in Europe again. Although they haven't made as big an impact as Rangers in recent seasons, they've definitely had their moments. Probably the most exciting period was our great UEFA Cup run in 1988 when we were eventually very unlucky to go out to a fine Bayern Munich side.

In the first round we overcame a difficult clash in Dublin against St Pat's, but once we got them back to Tynecastle there was never any doubt about the result.

The next hurdle, against Austria Vienna was going to be a real step up, but they were two great ties. We drew 0–0 at Tynecastle and a lot of people wrote us off and thought we had no real chance of winning; but we were playing well and had a lot of confidence that season and we knew if we performed to our best we had a chance.

The trip over there was something else. The chairman had chartered a DC10 which I nearly refused to fly in, but the hotel made up for it. It was one of the finest hotels I've ever been in and made Gleneagles or Turnberry look like a b&b.

If there was a real hero of that season it had to be Mike Galloway and he duly grabbed the vital goal to put us through.

It's hard to believe, but it was Walter Kidd of all people who beat the offside trap and sent in a great cross which Mike got on the end of to spark celebrations which continued long into the night.

Mike proved to be a great buy. He scored a lot of goals in Europe and could play in a number of positions, at the back, midfield or up front which he did to great effect.

Another vital match was the home leg of our clash with Velez Mostar when Eamonn Bannon and John Colquhoun grabbed three crucial goals which more or less guaranteed our quarter-final spot, while we did well at the back to keep a clean sheet.

Personally I'm modest enough to think that the away leg in Austria was one of my best ever Euro performances and I was really relishing the Bayern match. It was a classic European night in front of a capacity Tynecastle crowd and the fans went wild when we won thanks to a scorching free-kick from Iain Ferguson, who's always been a player for the big occasion. After that the supporters expected us to beat them in Germany . . . and they were very nearly right.

We got off to a great start when John Colquhoun broke through and just about demolished the posts with a sizzling shot. The keeper actually made a great fingertip save to push it on to the woodwork, but we didn't get a corner for it. I had a shot cleared off the line and we were looking good until Bayern hit us on the break and our dream was over. We were all gutted, especially as we would have faced Napoli in the next round. Just how good our performances were was shown the next season when Rangers lost convincingly home and away to the Germans.

An unforgettable moment of that trip came on the flight home. The stewardess told everyone 'please don't walk about the cabin while the seatbelt sign is on,' but before the 'thankyou' and a bing-bong, the ego had landed. The chairman, who'd already managed to get the club fined thousands in a dispute over the sale of TV rights which broke UEFA rules, had decided these rules didn't apply to him either and strutted up to the front of the plane and grabbed the mike.

'I'd like to thank every one of you Hearts fans for following the team in Europe and thank the players for their efforts,' he said as the cabin crew looked on in amazement. Ten minutes later, we were nearly on the ground anyway when he sat down to a round of applause. Wallace was bad enough in Scotland but can you imagine him on the loose in Europe? I'm surprised he didn't light up a cigar while he was there!

Alex MacDonald was in the Jock Wallace mould of European tacticians. He would switch some things round during games if he had to, but his attitude was usually to put the best possible team on the park and say, 'Right, go out and give it your best shot,' which we tried to do.

Nights like that in places like the Olympic stadium and at home are magic, occasions which every player savours. Although there have been some notable performances from Scottish teams in recent years, especially from Dundee United and Aberdeen, we should be doing better on a more regular basis.

If Munich was a highlight, my worst experience with the Jam Tarts has to be against Bologna a couple of seasons ago when we beat them 3–1 at home and then crashed 3–0 away.

Although nobody likes to miss out on big games like these, one trip I was glad I didn't make was to Dnepr. It was a closed city for years and we were the first foreigners to go there in the post-glasnost era. The lads told me it was atrocious. The food and accommodation were terrible and to a man they were overjoyed to be home. The boss did me a good turn by not making me go even though I was suspended, and the rest must have done me good as I scored our first goal in the return tie.

It's a great bonus for the club to be taking part in European competition again and qualifying for either the Cup-Winners' Cup or UEFA Cup, has to be our target, though we'd all love a crack at the Champions' League some day. Aberdeen and Dundee United flew the flag for Scotland in the eighties, so who's to say that Hearts can't be standard-bearers as we head towards the end of the century?

Admittedly we took a pounding in Belgrade at the start of this season, but a 0–0 draw over there was a great start to our Cup-Winners' Cup campaign. I was delighted with my own performance and Gilles Rousset had a tremendous night, pulling off some magnificent stops.

I had a real scare before the second leg when I fell ill the following Sunday and was later diagnosed as having pleurisy.

After some antibiotics and a rest I felt well enough to train the following week and not only played but scored a first-half goal to keep our hopes alive.

I was delighted with that, but I'd have been even happier if it had been enough to take us through to the next round. Losing a second-half goal meant we went out on the away goals rule despite another battling team display.

Red Star beat Rangers not so long ago and even though the team has changed, they still had a lot of quality players in their side. A lot of people didn't notice, but at the end of the game, you would have thought the Slavs had won the Cup Winners Cup the way they celebrated. Obviously they knew they'd been in a fight and respected Rangers as tough opponents and we've got to take some comfort from that.

I don't see any reason why Hearts can't make it back into Europe next season. We've got a stronger squad than last year, but first we've got to do the business in the League and finish as high up the table as possible.

13

DERBY DAYS

When it comes to sheer excitement and passion, there's nothing to beat derby matches, regardless of the scoreline. And having played in both the Glasgow and Edinburgh fixtures, it's a stock question to compare the two.

The answer's simple – you can't. For the fans and players of all four clubs a victory over their city rivals means everything and makes for a great Saturday night when, unusually, they can't wait to get to work on a Monday to share the moment with workmates who were at the opposite end of the ground.

An Old Firm derby, is without doubt a bigger occasion, simply because the respective stadiums have a larger capacity. They are without doubt the biggest two clubs in the country and the religious divide is at its widest in the west of Scotland.

I must have been involved in over sixty derby clashes over the years, and I've loved every one since I made my Old Firm debut on 23 March 1982 in front of 51,000 at Parkhead, which I can just about remember as being a fairly open game, despite finishing 0–0. One of those early clashes was even more special because it brought my first winner's medal.

The date was 25 March 1984. After the disappointment of being dropped by John Greig for another League Cup final against Celtic and then being on the losing side in the Scottish Cup against Aberdeen, the chance finally to lift a Cup at Hampden was a tremendous prospect.

We'd had a rough time against a fairly strong Celtic squad with guys like Charlie Nicholas and Brian McClair doing a lot of damage, but under big Jock we were really fired up for the match that Sunday. Ally McCoist finally made his mark with a hat-trick in an epic final which no one who was there will ever forget.

Ally gave us the lead from a first-half penalty and grabbed another to put us two up. But then, after Brian McClair had pulled one back for the Celts, Coisty managed to give away a penalty with just a minute to go when he brought down Murdo MacLeod. He swears to this day that Bob Valentine got it wrong. Mark Reid equalised to send the game into extra-time, but things swung back our way when another penalty was awarded, this time to us. I think all the spot-kick incidents were more clumsy than anything else. This time Roy Aitken barged Ally on the edge of the box and I think having given Celtic the decision in the dying seconds of normal time, the referee had no real option but to give us the shout this time. I wasn't bothered about whether it was a soft decision or not, and neither was Ally. Pat Bonner actually saved his spot kick, but as the Celtic fans roared he followed up to send the Ibrox legions into ecstasy.

It was a really special day. Old Firm games at either Parkhead or Ibrox are huge affairs, but in front of 66,000 at Hampden there was an even better atmosphere. When you first run out of the tunnel you try to blank out the crowd, then at the end, if you've won, you go to your own fans to celebrate; if you've lost you get off the pitch as quickly as possible.

For the record, the team that day was: McCloy, Nicholl, Dawson, McClelland, Paterson, McPherson, Russell, McCoist, Clark (McAdam), MacDonald (Burns), Cooper.

I'd already won a Glasgow Cup medal, which is actually one of the nicer medals even though it's not as important as the others, thanks to a Sandy Clark goal but this was even more special.

Before that Coisty entered the record books for scoring at Parkhead in 27 seconds in August 1983, although Frank McGarvey found the net with four minutes to go to give them the win. There was a slight hint of offside about Ally's tap-in after we hit them on the break from the kick-off. But he certainly didn't care and neither did we. It was real end-to-end stuff before Frank scored. He was one of the toughest strikers to play against as he'd run straight at you and you never knew what was coming next.

Another exciting derby under Jock was the April fixture when Bobby Williamson scored with a great overhead kick. Jimmy Nicholl, who was making his farewell appearance before he went back to Toronto Blizzard, was sent off and Craig Paterson, John McClelland and I had our hands full, but successfully held out against the Celtic attack.

Then of course came the unbelievable 4–4 game at Ibrox. That was incredible stuff. You felt as if both teams were capable of scoring every time they went up the park. On a greasy surface mistakes were going to be made and the fans must have been shell-shocked after it – I know the players were.

Cammy Fraser had a bit of a rough time from the fans, especially after giving a section of them the V sign following a bit of heckling. But after scoring twice against our oldest rivals he was elevated to hero status. After going behind, we scored three times in 11 minutes and led 4–3 with 20 minutes to go when Murdo MacLeod blasted in a terrific 30-yard strike to grab a share of the points. I was marking wee Mo who made a run and cut inside before passing to Murdo. It was one of the best games I've ever played in, although the best ones are always the ones you win.

One of the last Old Firm matches I was involved in turned out to be one of the most exciting. For years we'd missed Celtic in the early stages of the Cup, but suddenly it was more or less expected that we would come out of the hat together. The Gers had a rough time of it in Graeme Souness's final season when they lost in the League and the Cup, but since then there had been the epic semi-final win with ten men which had taken them to their first Scottish Cup win, against Airdrie, in 11 years. That was the season before I re-signed for them.

Following our fantastic treble-winning season of 1992–93 we scored another ten-man success against them in the semi-final of the League Cup in September 1993. This time the Ranger heading for an early bath was Dutch winger Piet Huistra who retaliated to a bad challenge and was red-carded early in the match.

But in a superb atmosphere, with Celtic fans occupying the whole of the Govan stand, we battled bravely and Mark Hateley grabbed the crucial goal after Ian Durrant had given Mike Galloway the slip and sent in a pinpoint cross. Our fans went absolutely wild and when we held on to book our place in the final against Hibs, the noise was absolutely unbelievable.

The down side to that kind of night is that you know that sooner or later you are going to end up on the losing side as well, though hopefully not as often. And just over a month later we looked as though we were cruising towards another win when we lost two late goals with Brian O'Neill scoring a later winner to give new boss Lou Macari a lift.

Walter slaughtered us for that one as we had been so far ahead in the match, but often in derby matches it isn't the team playing the best football that wins the match.

I never did manage to score against Celtic in all those clashes even though I've managed it a couple of times for Hearts, but in the Edinburgh derby, along with Robbo, I've not got a bad scoring record. Last season I managed to get on the scoresheet again.

It was a typical derby with one team doing all the tackling and getting to the ball first. We were shooting down the Easter Road slope which is always a nightmare and makes it the proverbial game of two halves. I much prefer a nice level pitch which plays the same for 90 minutes.

We made a great start with the old McPherson–Robertson combination paying dividends again. Robbo got the ball first and delivered a great cross from the right which I met with a diving header at the back post – the only diving header I think I've ever scored.

I got the customary stick off the Hibs fans for scoring which only makes you play even harder, then I ran back towards our fans and it was great to see the delight on their faces. It's always great to score, but to do it in a derby is even better as there is more significance attached to the result.

Unfortunately we let them back into the match and they scored twice, but in the dying seconds I went up for a free-kick, managed to get a touch on it and put the defence off, leaving Mr Derby himself to rattle it in for a draw as the ref blew for full-time almost immediately.

The biggest difference between the derbies is that when you arrive at Easter Road at a quarter to two, the streets round the ground and the stadium itself are very quiet. At Ibrox or Parkhead when you go out for a pre-match pitch inspection there are thousands already in the ground and the nearby streets are a throng of blue and green hours before the kick-off.

I'd done well in derbies in my first spell at Hearts, but I started with a bang in my second spell. The match was due to be played at the New Year, but because the pitch was waterlogged it was rearranged for the middle of the month.

Surprise, surprise, it was another header, this time at the front post from a corner. John Millar went on to score the winner.

At the time we had gone over 20 matches without losing against the Hibbies. That's a great boost for a long while when you think 'we can't lose', but like every unbeaten run there comes a time when you also think 'this can't go on for ever'. Once it's crossed your mind, it's usually not too long before you do suffer a defeat.

Of course, having Robbo in the team is usually worth at least a goal start because of the terrific record he has against Hibs. He's scored a few classic goals, but one that always sticks in my mind was when John burst through, Alan Rough, the Hibs keeper at the time, came off his line, John coolly rounded him and then finished from a really tight angle.

Not at all bad for a man who was brought up as a Hibby!

14

SURVIVAL SKILLS

In October 1994 it was time to hit the road again – back along the M8 to Tynecastle as part of a deal which saw Alan McLaren head in the opposite direction and promising Ibrox youngster David Hagen join me at Hearts.

If it had been all change at Ibrox when I returned there, it was a similar story at Tynecastle. For a start there was no Wallace Mercer, Chris Robinson having taken over as chairman, the ground had undergone a facelift and there was a new manager, Tommy McLean having taken over from Sandy Clark. The club's fortunes had also been up and down during the two years I'd been gone, but there were still a few familiar faces like Robbo, Craig Levein, Gary Mackay, John Colquhoun and Neil Berry.

After Joe Jordan left for Parkhead, the last manager under Wallace Mercer was my old Ibrox and Hearts team-mate Sandy Clark. But he was faced with the same problems as his predecessors, no cash and no real chance of getting any to spend. He brought in the crop of youngsters who had done so well for the club the previous season, but while they matured the club's fortunes gradually declined. The club found itself among the relegation candidates for a spell, although they eventually dug deep to earn a Premier Division reprieve.

Sandy was a very popular choice and was respected by all the players under him, but even Mercer himself reckoned he needed more time, something he was denied as he became the first casualty in the boardroom battle that saw Mercer ousted. I gather that Sandy is still very bitter about the way things turned out, especially as the club is now reaping the benefits of his youth policy. I think he found it hard to take the step up at the beginning, but eventually he did what every manager has to do and gained the respect of the players. By then, though, it was too late to make amends that season. Had he been given longer he would undoubtedly have learned from any mistakes.

Chris Robinson and co then made what was greeted at the time as a sound move in appointing Tommy McLean, who had fallen out with Motherwell after years of sterling service. But for a variety of reasons, the switch didn't work out and Tommy had a relatively short term of office in the Gorgie hotseat.

I'd known Tommy since we were both at Ibrox together. He was coming to the end of a career during which he had won every domestic honour in the game and a European Cup Winners Cup medal, while I was taking my first steps on the professional ladder. When Greigsy resigned he was my boss briefly. I was looking forward to coming back to Hearts and working under him again, especially with the reputation he had gained as manager of Motherwell. Like the rest of our squad, I had the greatest respect for the way he built a Motherwell side which went from being perennial relegation candidates, to a team capable of challenging for the league title and of course the Scottish Cup. I knew the way he trained players and that he was very tactically minded with a great knowledge of the game.

But as soon as I got there, I realised something wasn't quite right. A few months later I read a newspaper article where he revealed that he had actually offered his resignation to the board, which I thought was very strange.

Throughout the season various bits of news filtered back to the dressing-room. It was rumoured that he and the chairman weren't on speaking terms and you could tell that he wasn't happy at the club. As a result the players became increasingly disenchanted.

I reckoned that, having enjoyed the relative security of his position at Fir Park, where he also had a seat on the board, he didn't really adjust to not having the same kind of clout and relationship with the directors. We all gave it our best shot, but on the park we were struggling and everyone knew something had to give.

When he first arrived there was an outcry from some sections of the support, who still remembered him as a member of the Kilmarnock side, who under Willie Waddell, had pipped Hearts for the league title in 1965. The disgruntled punters complained that he wasn't a 'Hearts man'. That was probably true, but for whatever reasons, I felt that he didn't settle at Tynecastle right from the word go.

Who knows? But his last days at Hearts were very unsettling for everyone at the club, not least Tam himself. A lot of players who had been at the club for a number of years, like Gary Mackay and John Robertson, who have been here a number of years, knew something had to give and felt that Tommy wasn't going to be there in the long-term, or even the short-term if it came to that.

Before I rejoined Hearts I had won five medals in the space of two seasons. Suddenly we were fighting for our Premier lives. The rest of the lads had gone through a similar experience the previous year under Sandy Clark. People say it's tough at the top but let me tell you it's even harder going at the bottom. You're under a totally different pressure. Being under pressure to win titles is ultimately far more enjoyable than a relegation battle at the opposite end of the table.

Tommy at times had a bit of a negative attitude which I think he passed on to Eamonn.

'This is going to happen . . . we're going to lose this game,' was the sort of doom and gloom we became used to.

One incident that speaks volumes for that period at Tynecastle was when Tommy decided to bring in a sports psychologist.

'I feel your confidence is down and I'd like you to have a session with this guy to see if he can help,' he told us.

We all agreed that we didn't need to speak to him.

'We're going through a bad spell, which happens in football, but we'll get ourselves out of it,' was our attitude.

Tam said okay and that appeared to be that. But a few days later he called a team meeting in one of the suites upstairs. When we walked in, the psychologist was sitting there. Now if Tam had asked the guy, he would probably have agreed that that in itself was a bad move, guaranteed to provoke a negative attitude to the whole idea. We'd been consulted, but then ignored. Tommy springing it on us was the wrong way to handle it. Right away we'd lost a bit of confidence in the manager who had in effect conned us. To us it should have been down to each individual to speak to someone like that. Some players may well have benefited, but it could have made others worse. Personally I didn't need it.

Even though we'd been put on the spot, we thought we'd give it a go for ten minutes. But eventually we convinced him that Tommy, who wasn't even in the room, was more in need of his services than us.

'Look, you shouldn't be speaking to us. We don't think we're going to lose, it's the manager! Why don't you speak to him.'

I think the guy did speak to Tommy, who was less than chuffed. We all knew there were things we had to sort out, but we all knew this wasn't the answer.

One of the worst days was losing to Airdrie in the semi-final of the Scottish Cup in April, with their striker Steve Cooper doing the damage.

Robbo was red-carded with five minutes to go, although to be fair to the Airdrie player involved, Tony Smith, who started his career at Tynecastle, he backed John afterwards, saying the ref had got it wrong. But that was little comfort at the time. We took a lot of stick from the fans after that one.

What made it even worse was that we had already done the hard work, defeating Rangers in the quarter-finals at Tynecastle. I scored the first goal and set up the fourth for Kevin Thomas after one of my famous lung-busting cavalry charges up the park in an epic cup tie, and probably our best result of the season. We were 2–0 up until Rangers battled their way back into it, and Robbo got the vital third goal. We had gone 17 games without defeating Rangers, but that Monday night made up for the previous disappointments.

Just as when I left Rangers for the first time, I definitely had something to prove and it's always good to score against them.

Having said that, I also knocked Hearts out of the Cup in 1993 at Parkhead with another goal, so if anyone ever needed proof that I'm a professional and give everything to whichever team I've been with, there's two very good examples.

A high spot was scoring in a victory over Hibs in a rearranged derby match.

And I scored again in a 2–1 defeat against Aberdeen, a match that if we'd won would almost certainly have sent them down.

One big change during Tommy's reign was the departure of Henry Smith. Henry came in for his fair share of stick during his long career with Hearts, but he holds the club record for appearances in the number 1 jersey and he was always a big favourite with the fans.

He was a very agile keeper and, off the park, a really nice, quiet, even shy, guy. But he used to scare the life out of me sometimes. You'd be chasing a long ball through and waiting for a shout from the keeper which never came. Then you'd glance up and he'd be about a millimetre away from you and give you the fright of your life. It's probably an understatement to say he wasn't the most vocal of goalkeepers.

He made some mistakes as we all do, but he pulled us out of a few holes in a lot of seasons and was a great shotstopper.

Everybody at Tynecastle that season gave their all to keep the club up. The lads told me it had been even tougher the previous season, but in the final matches results elsewhere worked in our favour and United took the fall, while Aberdeen survived by the skin of their teeth.

It was probably the worst season I've ever experienced in all my years in football, and certainly not one I'd ever fancy repeating. And even though Tommy had kept us up, the writing was on the wall and he was replaced by Jim Jefferies in the close season.

15

TOP GUNS

I've had the privilege of forming a goalscoring partnership with two of the most prolific strikers in Scottish football whose record-breaking and memorable goals far outstrip my own modest tally.

Ally McCoist and John Robertson are without doubt two of the most gifted goalscorers of modern times, and I can reveal that at one stage Robbo came close to joining Ally in the blue of Rangers.

John has never hidden the fact that he would have loved to have played for Rangers and had the same opportunities as Ally, even though he's a closet Hibby.

Yep, that's two exclusives in the one chapter, even though it's hard to believe that the man who's scored more than 20 goals in Edinburgh derbies was a Hibbies fan as a kid! Luckily for us he signed for Hearts as a schoolboy and was converted from then on in.

If Graeme Souness had had his way, John and Ally might have teamed up together at Ibrox. Now that would have been a prolific partnership, although there would probably have been a punch-up every time a penalty was awarded!

The deal was all set to go through until Rangers found themselves under investigation for tapping another player. League rules state that clubs have to deal directly, but of course it happens all the time. If everyone was to play it straight no one would ever move.

John was disappointed at the time, but he was pleased that Souness and Smith had shown interest and he's gone on to score even more goals for Hearts.

Robbo isn't the fastest or fittest striker, but his record in the

Premier League is tremendous. Never mind running, even if he couldn't walk, he'd still score goals. He's got an eye for goal and you'll never take that away from him.

Over the years, managers have tried to make him work hard, tried to get him fitter. I mean he hardly looks like a lethal goalscoring machine.

But Ally McCoist still takes the same kind of stick, and his record is second to none. I've played against and with strikers who are fitter and faster than both, but lack the predatory instincts Robbo and Coisty have.

Fans tend to look at faults rather than strengths and judge not on how many a striker has scored but on how many he should have scored.

During my time at Rangers I nearly lost count of the number of strikers and the millions of pounds spent on replacements for Ally. During Souness's time alone the likes of Colin West, Mark Falco, Mo Johnston and Mark Hateley all came and went having enjoyed varying degrees of success. Coisty's still there and so is Robbo.

When John was sold to Newcastle, Hearts had a string of would-be successors, without success, before the wee man came back from St James's in 1988 and started banging them in again.

Nobody needs reminding of the Golden Boots and records Ally's bagged, but Robbo has also topped the Premier Division scoring charts, in 1989–90 and has been Hearts' top scorer a dozen times since he banged in 21 goals in the First Division in the 1983–84 season.

They'd probably disagree, but I'm convinced that psychologically it's a good thing. They've dug their heels in and are able to say 'I'm a better striker than him, I've scored more goals, always will, and they can't get rid of me.' Of course, there will come a time when that's no longer the case, but both of them have a few match-winners left in them over the next few seasons.

Playing for a club like Rangers, over the season and over 90 minutes you do get a lot more chances created, so a hitman of John's ability would undoubtedly have scored even more goals than he already has.

John always worried about the club looking for replacements for him, but to me his fears were totally unfounded. I told him, 'Look, to replace you they'll have to get someone even better – and I can't see anyone who can fill your boots, so don't worry about it.'

That didn't stop him worrying though. Strikers in particular have to handle a lot of strain mentally and John's a bit of a confidence man. When things are going well for him and he's scoring goals he's very chirpy, but uncertainties and criticism do affect his confidence.

Moving back down the pitch, another one of the best players I've had the pleasure to play alongside and against is Andy Goram. I don't think anyone in Scotland, or even Europe comes close to having his class. There are goalkeepers who will save you in certain circumstances, but for consistency and the ability to pull off the kind of stops that will keep you in a game, Andy's definitely the man.

He doesn't look like the most athletic goalie, and I'm sure he won't mind me saying that. But appearances don't matter – it's how you perform on the park that matters and he's a tremendous goalkeeper to play in front of.

He's not a keeper who comes for every cross, but as long as you know what he's going to do it helps you as well. If you have a keeper who sometimes comes for high balls and sometimes doesn't, then you can be a bit hesitant yourself as you try to work out his next move. With Andy you always know exactly what he's going to do and it's quite easy to read the situation.

He also does a lot of shouting. He's very vocal . . . especially at the bar! I've had a lot of laughs with Andy with Rangers and Scotland but he's not a man you want to upset either.

During one of my first games back with Rangers, things weren't going too well and there was a bit of a fracas at half-time. Andy and Nigel Spackman had words and the next minute Andy had jumped up off his seat in the dressing-room, ready to smack Nigel right in the kisser. He can be very volatile, but only because he's got a great attitude and wants to keep a clean sheet and win every game. If things aren't going according to plan, he lets you know about it.

He's very strong in the air and protects himself well as plenty of forwards who've had the misfortune to collide with him accidentally or otherwise, will tell you. He stands his ground every time and the only time I've seen him coming off second best was when we played Club Brugge in the Champions' League in 1992–93 when I banged into him and flattened him!

Because he's the Scotland and Rangers number 1 Andy's always in the spotlight and attracts more than his fair share of unwanted media attention. But it's easy to get the wrong impression of him. He's a great guy and a real character in the dressing-room, one of the players that every club would love to have. He's very funny, can be a bit of a timebomb occasionally, but that's just his character and you wouldn't want to change that.

Having been the only player in recent times to have two separate spells at Ibrox, I've been lucky to have played alongside two great wingers, tremendous talents from different eras of Rangers' success, in Davie Cooper and Brian Laudrup. It's a real tragedy that we'll never see them on the same pitch. Coop didn't have the pace that Brian has, but he certainly had the flair and imagination. On his day he could have played with any team in the world.

He teed up so many goals for others and scored some classics himself, like his free-kick in the Skol Cup final against Aberdeen and the classic against Celtic in the Dryborough Cup not long after he joined Rangers.

The £100,000 Clydebank got to let him go in 1977 was a terrific bit of business. If it was 0–0 and you desperately needed a goal, Davie was the man you would expect to produce a little bit of magic. Players like that are hard to come by. In training he was exactly the same as during a match. He hated the fitness work, and just couldn't wait to get the ball and rip up a couple of defenders. He was a real joy to play with and a great passer of the ball. I can remember a number of occasions in my early days at Ibrox when you would push forward, make a pass and carry on looking for the return. For a defender there's nothing worse than going forward to make a pass and never seeing the ball again. But Coop always found you.

He was involved in one my most embarrassing moments though. I broke out of defence, played a one–two with Davie and spotting Hibs' goalie Alan Rough on the 18-yard line chipped the ball with the outside of my foot and turned away to celebrate what I thought was a classic goal as the ball was heading straight for the middle of the net. I was a bit miffed when none of my team-mates ran to join in the celebrations and even more upset when the Hibs striker told me, 'Davie, the ball didn't go in.'

I saw it later on TV and discovered I'd hit it with a bit too much spin. It had landed on the line and rolled in the opposite direction. You can't hide at Ibrox and I just wanted the ground to open up. Fortunately the fans saw the funny side and I didn't take too much stick.

Coop got a new lease of life when Graeme Souness arrived at Ibrox. They were in the Scots squad for the World Cup in Mexico in 1986 and had a mutual respect and admiration for each other's talents. Davie rated Souness as the world-class player he was and vice versa.

Davie came back from Mexico a totally different player and went on to have a great first season under Graeme. He did as much as anyone to help bring back that elusive league title.

Coop would moan if training was too hard and then turn round the following week and complain that it was too easy. He's very similar to Hearts' John Colquhoun in that respect. But he only did it for effect. He always liked to wind people up and get a response. Consequently, he never quite shook off the Albert Tatlock nickname, after the grumpy *Coronation Street* character, but he did lose his other Moody Blue tag earned for his infrequent chats with the press. With Souness at the helm he opened up a bit, became more outgoing and more approachable.

That was a process that continued right up until his untimely death. He eventually finished his playing days with Motherwell and as he continued to mellow, he even started enjoying coaching, something he had always hated as a young player, and looked set for a move in that direction.

Even now, it's hard to believe he's gone. I'm sure a new generation of fans will continue to appreciate his skills on video.

Those fans already have a new hero in Brian Laudrup and it's not just in Scotland either. Ally is a big star here with fans of all ages, but Brian is a real national hero in Denmark as we discovered on a preseason trip there when he was mobbed everywhere we went. Brian's skill and his image and attitude off the park have made him a real hit over there. He's probably the most gifted player we have in Scotland right now and on top form he's a natural successor to Davie Cooper.

People have accused him of being a Serie A reject, because he didn't stay on in Italy. But Brian and Pasquale Bruno have told me a few stories about the Fiorentina fans, tales of players having to leave the stadium in a car boot after being besieged by angry mobs after a defeat.

They said the fans were absolutely crazy about the team and didn't take too kindly to defeats at all. Now you get paid to play football, not for being under that kind of constant pressure and I think Brian found it very difficult, especially for his family. It's maybe easier if you're there on your own, but if your kids have to put up with it as well, it's a different story. It's also fair to say that Lauders, as he's known at Ibrox, isn't the most physical of players and the cynicism of Italian defenders was another factor in his decision to quit Italy.

From the time Denis Law did a bunk from Torino in the sixties there have been a string of stars who've failed to adapt to the obsessive attitude that Italian fans, press and club owners regard as normal.

There have been success stories like Mark Hateley and Ray Wilkins with AC Milan and Graeme Souness with Sampdoria, but even big Mark wasn't without his fair share of problems during his term there. Having seen both sides of the coin, he was instrumental in persuading Brian to sign on at Ibrox.

Brian's got the ability to play in any league in the world, but he's thriving in Scotland. Even if he were to leave Rangers, there would be a queue of Premier clubs eager for his signature. He's happy here and that's obviously what counts.

Like the rest of us, though, he may find the main drawback in Scotland is the sheer monotony of playing the same teams and opponents on a near-constant basis.

I've played with and against Mo Johnston over the years and I have to say I enjoyed playing against him. Mo's a top striker, but along with other top Scots strikers like Davie Dodds, Andy Gray and even Coisty, you get to know them too well. Familiarity in this case breeds boredom because you play them so often, a minimum of four times a season, year after year in some cases. You know what runs they're going to make; you know exactly when they're going to be physical and when you have to be physical towards them. It's not hard, it's just repetitive. Sure, they'll still score goals against you, but to be honest the most difficult opponents I've ever had have all been foreign. They're the ones you really have to watch, when you have to keep your concentration at 100 per cent.

Two that spring to mind are the first two continental stars of that quality that I faced, Inter Milan's Karl-Heinz Rummenigge and Altobelli.

Playing in front of 65,000 in the San Siro in the UEFA Cup in 1984 was a fantastic experience, even if we did lose. It was a great night for me but that pairing, who had starred for Germany and Italy in the 1982 World Cup provided a real education.

They were a couple of real speed merchants – not just in terms of whether or not they would beat you over 100 yards (which they probably would), but for sheer quick thinking, timing runs to perfection and making space for themselves brilliantly.

On the night Rummenigge scored a magnificent overhead kick and I was close to applauding it myself when it was disallowed – for having his boot up and dangerous play!

Altobelli simply oozed class. When he got the ball at his feet, it was superglued there. He used his weight to shield the ball superbly and there was no danger you were going to get it back off him, unless you gave away a foul.

The lessons were simple. You had to be every bit as sharp as them, stay one step ahead and read the situation just as quickly.

Another star of that side was Franco Baresi. Everyone has a player they like to model themselves on and I was a huge fan of Baresis. It was a great experience to play against him so early in my career.

Another of the real legends I've had the privilege to share a pitch with was the great Johan Cruyff when Feyenoord played at Ibrox in the KLM Cup – and I managed to nutmeg him! I couldn't believe I'd managed that, but, mind you, Jock made me man-mark him and I have to admit I didn't get closer than five yards for most of the match. I wasn't overawed during the game, but after it I was too nervous to ask him to swap jerseys. Just being there was enough, especially when he shook my hand and said 'well done'.

At international level, when I eventually made the breakthrough, you simply don't come across players of the quality of Brazilians like Carecas.

In the European Championships it's fantastic to be able to test yourself and be on the same pitch as players like Marco Van Basten and Ruud Gullit. That Dutch side was maybe fading slightly around that time, with both of them plagued by injury, but for my money it was still one of the world's best ever striking partnerships.

You can try being physical with guys like that, but it won't get you far. They're well used to that in Italy and they're not going to be intimidated easily. You just have to concentrate on getting the ball. The way to upset them is to try to be that split second sharper in your own reading of the game. That's when you affect their confidence. They'll try to make space for themselves, but if you've read it right and got there first it throws them a bit and they'll then switch to plan B.

It is a bit of a cliché, but playing at that level on a regular basis really sharpens you up.

Of course, then you come back to Scotland and you know exactly where the ball's going, so it's more of a physical than mental battle again. Any player who tells you that's not the case, barring maybe half a dozen games over the course of the season, is telling porkies. I've spoken to a few and they all agree it's not.

So for that reason, playing in Europe, getting the chance to expand your knowledge of the game and experience something new which will test you to the limit always leaves a bigger impression. Once you get a taste of that you want it again and again and I would really love to see a European league in the future, even if I don't have the chance to play in it myself.

The player who's made the biggest impact this season with his wonder hat-trick is Ally McCoist. But the other side of him is his undisputed role as the Ibrox court jester. He was ably assisted, and in a lot of cases upstaged, by Durranty, who when paired with Derek Ferguson could be even more of a handful. Durranty and Fergie are two of the best players ever to wear a blue jersey, and they stuck together off and on the park.

Among my earliest memories of that double act is yet another away day, this time a break to Malta. The two of them were full of beans all the time and brilliant to have around, especially at that age. They remind me of two youngsters at Hearts just now, Gary Naismith and John Paul Burns who are great friends off the park and stick up for each other all the time.

Anyway, we had a couple of days off in Malta and someone had the bright idea of hiring a car. The only ones available were old-fashioned British models and, having just passed my test and being a bit slow, I did the hiring. That meant I had to stay sober and drive up to a maximum of ten players crammed into a vintage Mini Clubman.

At one stage in the night, Durrant and Ferguson discovered that no one in Malta locks their cars because they're so old. As it turned out the car's age was a real plus point – you couldn't see the bumps as the Blues Brothers proceeded to let off as many handbrakes on hills as they could and play their own abridged version of stock car racing. Eventually we got them back under control, or so we thought, Mr Sensible here doing 20 miles an hour with Durranty covering my eyes and Fergie trying to strangle me.

They've calmed down a bit since then, fortunately and after making their debuts under Jock they went on to produce a great midfield partnership.

They were totally different players. Derek was more in the Ray Wilkins mould, a great passer of the ball, with great vision and a great touch, probably the best I've seen apart from Laudrup. Like Ian he was very unlucky with injury, but he was still a great player when he arrived at Hearts and I enjoyed teaming up with him again. He's got marvellous technical ability and when he played well so did the team. He's the type of player you can give the ball to anywhere on the pitch with as many opponents round him as you like and he'll still control it and make a pass. He rarely gives the ball away.

Durranty was faster and made a lot of penetrating runs and scored a lot of valuable goals. A lot of people thought he was finished after his devastating injury, but he's still capable of turning it on at the top level, although there's no telling just how good he could have been if it hadn't been for those missing years.

Another who deserves a mention in the midfield area is Hearts' Gary Mackay. He's been terrific for Hearts in all the years he's been at Tynecastle and, of course, he's a diehard Jambo who's never wanted anything other than to pull on a Hearts jersey every Saturday. Despite that he's still come in for a bit of criticism from the Gorgie faithful, but he's been the real mainstay of some quality Hearts teams.

He's played over 600 games and scored a lot of important goals. He made his debut for Hearts at a very young age and the fact that he's lasted so long under a succession of managers speaks volumes for him and his commitment to the club.

He plays very well off the front two. He's got a great understanding with Robbo which has paid off more than a few times and both have scored a lot of goals through that.

Gary's talents have also been recognised at international level and he's probably best remembered for his goal against Bulgaria which got the Republic of Ireland to the World Cup in America. We were over in Dublin recently for a couple of pre-season games and Gary's still remembered fondly over there for that.

Off the park he's a really nice guy, but even now after all those games, he's still a bit paranoid about whether he's playing or not. He's always first to check the team list and even if he's on it, he scrutinises the side to see how far his name is up or down on the list. If it's at the bottom he probably won't sleep that night.

Not that sleeping is normally a problem with him. He goes to bed at eight o'clock every Friday night and prepares meticulously for every game. Everyone else stays in on a Friday too, but we only head for our kip when we're tired; not Gary. He's a bit of a worrier, but he's been a great servant to Hearts

16

KINGS OF THE CASTLE

After 35 barren years without a trophy, hopefully this will be the season that finally ends Hearts' typecasting as also-rans. We're the club that has produced more horror stories than Stephen King's back catalogue and so many unhappy endings we should be sponsored by Kleenex: Dens Park and Hampden in 1986, more semi-finals than I care to remember and more second prizes than any supporters deserve.

The club may be at the beginning of a new era, one where we can compete with the riches, in terms of cash and talent, that the Old Firm enjoys. But the jury's out at the moment and even though Jim Jefferies has led us to our first Cup final in ten years and got us back into Europe, there's a lot of hard work ahead for everyone if we're to build on that and take some silverware back to Tynecastle.

The post-Bosman era is throwing up new challenges for every club in Europe. Hearts and Scottish football as a whole have to adapt to survive, never mind compete at the highest level. The contract and transfer system is the biggest talking point at the moment, but I think in conjunction with this league reconstruction is needed again.

A lot of people claim that the game needs more rationalisation and that just about everyone outside of the Old Firm should be amalgamating.

Even though this might make business sense, football is so unlike any other business, I don't believe it will happen.

Personally, I would like to see *more* clubs in the Premier Division which I reckon could comfortably cope with 16 teams. Playing sides like Falkirk, Partick Thistle, Dundee United, Dunfermline, Morton and Dundee would be better than playing the same old faces time and again.

It's a joke for players with top clubs. The more success you have the slimmer your chances in every competition.

If you're involved in European competition be it the Champions' League, the UEFA Cup or Cup Winners Cup you might even have a preliminary round to play before the league season kicks off. Then you're straight into the League Cup. If you do well in that and get a run in the Scottish Cup after Christmas, it's Saturday and Wednesday games almost from the first whistle.

The game has to change for the better. The players having a bit more power in the wake of the Bosman ruling may help shape things for the future. But already we're seeing the same old insular attitude of Scottish football coming to the fore.

When I signed my first contract I was on a hiding to nothing. For a start, it was four against one. With the chairman, manager, assistant manager and director sitting across the table, how can you ever hope to negotiate a fair deal? They told you what you were getting and that was it. Now the power has shifted, maybe temporarily, but what we have to realise is that we are competing in a European market and we have to try to improve our standards here in Scotland.

For years, Scottish clubs have been snapping up players on freedom of contract from Europe and they've kept quiet about it. Now suddenly, there's a chance for Scottish players to have the same kind of freedom of movement as their Dutch or French counterparts and they're up in arms!

Jim Jefferies has already brought in Pasquale from Italy. Aberdeen have been plundering the rich seam of talent in the Netherlands and further afield.

But the transfer system and contractual situation here is still archaic. How many players are unhappy at clubs and should have the right to move on when there contract is up? But some, like Chris Honor and Miodrag Krivokapic when he was with Dundee United, have found themselves in no-man's land, with the club hanging on to their registration even if they've decided they want to move on. Again the players can end up making moves which might not suit them, but certainly suit the clubs.

I hope the mood of change in the game at the moment will benefit everyone and I include Hearts in that. We're ideally placed to stake a claim for a successful future in the seasons ahead.

One thing I like about Tynecastle is that the executive suites aren't as big as at Ibrox so you tend to get to know the people there a lot better. It's a very welcoming club. I kept a lot of friends from my first spell even when I went back to Rangers. They gave me some stick, but they've forgiven me now I've come back to Tynecastle.

Ibrox, with it's famous red-brick front, the marble staircase and the wood panelled dressing-rooms hasn't changed a lot since the days of Alan Morton, Willie Waddell and Jim Baxter. The history and tradition of the club is still there. At Tynecastle it's not as powerful, but it's still there and it's not changed much over the years.

It's good to see the new stand up with more to come. There was talk of building another stadium elsewhere and even groundsharing at Murrayfield, which would have been excellent, but it's not home and I'm quite glad that we've stayed in Gorgie.

Once the other two stands are built it will be a very imposing stadium. Its already started to get like that and it's only half finished. In the next couple of years I'm sure any team coming to Tynecastle will enjoy the atmosphere. I watched a reserve game recently and even for that there was a big turnout and a good atmosphere. The Hearts support are always behind us in any season. The numbers fall off a bit during a run of bad results, but there's a great tradition of support that runs through generations of grandads, dads and sons and even grannies, daughters and granddaughters, something which is very much encouraged at Hearts and is great to see.

We held an open day at the end of last season. The club put up a big marquee and all the players were there. It was amazing just how much of a family affair it was. With Rangers it would have been the hard core of support, the bears, who would have turned up, but at Hearts there are more families.

The Great Waldo, or Wireless Mercer, as he was known after he got his own radio show, had more nicknames than most football club chairmen, but then again he was unlike most of that breed. He was a flamboyant character and definitely had an ego, but he was an expert at getting the club a lot of publicity and a higher profile. He was also the man who kept Hearts alive.

There's a picture hanging at Tynecastle of the Millerhill site on which, if he had got the planning permission and if he had succeeded in his takeover battle for Hibs, there would now be an absolutely unbelievable stadium. Underneath it someone has written 'Wallace's Pipe Dream'. Not a fan obviously, but I wonder how many people who maybe thought along similar lines at the time, still feel the same way now that we've got a new stadium being developed albeit at Tynecastle.

The current board of Chris Robinson, Leslie Deans, Fraser Jackson, Colin Wilson, John Frame and Ian McCallum are doing their best for the club, but they're hampered by the same problems as before. They're still in debt at the moment and need more cash to finance the ground redevelopment before they can even think about trying to match Rangers or Celtic in the transfer market. The 6,000-seater stand has already cost £2.8 million.

The share issue was a disappointment and raised nothing like the £1 million the club had hoped for, but hopefully the problems they face will be eradicated in time.

Every one of the guys on the board is a Hearts fan and they want the best for the club, as did the previous regime who gave it their best shot. A different approach is needed for different times and good performances on the pitch can bring even more supporters through the turnstiles and generate even more commercial income.

When I came back to Hearts I said to myself that I wanted to finish my career here, which I hope will happen. After that I like to think I'll have a future in coaching and management and be able to pass on what I've learned over the years under four managers at Rangers and the five I've played for at Hearts. I'm due to take my first SFA coaching badge and after that hope to develop that side of things gradually. It's something I've thought a lot about over the last few years and the more I thought the more I realised I want to give it a go.

I might not be any good at it. I've seen really talented players not make it as a boss, while the flip side is someone like Walter Smith who's won far more silverware as a manager than he ever did as a player.

But I've got enough confidence in my own abilities to think that I could be successful. A lot of ex-players go straight into management, but I'd prefer to work my way up, build up some coaching experience first. Whatever happens, I'll take it as it comes and give it my best shot, as I've always done as a player.

When the time comes to hang up my boots, I'll know, and I won't have any regrets. Some players have jacked it in too early and never forgiven themselves for it, but I'll know when the time is right. My contract with Hearts is up at the end of the season and although I know I can do a job for another couple of years at least, that's up to the manager. If I stay in the game and I'm still involved on a day-to-day basis and training I don't think I'll miss playing.

But just like leaving a club, I've never been scared to make a decision and stick by it. I'll play until I can't perform at a high level any more and I know it's stupid going out there. Having played in the Premier Division for my whole career, I don't fancy dropping down the Divisions and playing in front of a few hundred people. I'd rather go out at the top.

Looking back, I've not done too badly for someone who a lot of people had reservations about, including John Greig who wanted me to have a career outside football as a safety net. My dad thought my two brothers, Jim and Andrew, were better than me, something that's happened to a lot of players. I've achieved more than I expected, but then again, I didn't really know what to expect at 16.

I wanted to play for the Rangers first team and that was it; I'd achieved everything as far as I was concerned. I didn't look too far ahead. But then as your horizons broaden I wanted to play for Scotland, but I never dreamed I'd go to the World Cup finals or the European Championship; just as I never dreamed that I'd be part of a treble-winning side which was the highlight in terms of my domestic career.

But the World Cup in Italy was special and meeting Pele there was just as big a thrill as playing against Johan Cruyff a few years earlier.

For that I owe a few people a lot of thanks. Every manager I've been under has been a great help, but Alex MacDonald deserves a special mention. He was a huge influence on me rebuilding my career after the disappointment of leaving Rangers. He was hard but fair and never slow to give you a pat on the back or a boot up the backside. Without his help I don't think I would have played for Scotland and, like every player who's been under him, I can't speak highly enough of him.

My first coaches at Ibrox, Stan Anderson, Joe Mason and Davie Provan were also a great influence and their hard work meant I was given the best possible apprenticeship in the game. Having played over 300 first-team games for both Rangers and Hearts, won 27 full caps as well as youth, Under-21 and B honours, and won four League Cup, three league championship medals and one Scottish Cup badge, they must have been doing something right.

One ambition I've got left is to win a medal with Hearts. It's hard to explain just how much it means to the Hearts fans. Either of the two Cups probably represents our best chance as I don't see us being able to compete with the Old Firm in the League at the moment. We'd need to create an unbelievable team and spend millions and that's going to be very difficult. Cups are a different matter. The big guns can be knocked out and we always fancy our chances at Tynecastle in any match.

What does my future hold? Well, that's up to Jim Jefferies, who I'm sure will continue to build his own team as every manager wants to do. He wasn't the boss who signed me, but I think I've done a good job for him so far and if I look after myself I'm sure I can continue to do so. I'm just happy to have made a good start to the season. I felt good in pre-season training and fitness is everything in football. If you're not fit, you're not going to play to the best of your ability.

I found that out last season when I was out injured and trying to come back was a real struggle. But if you've got your fitness you play well and if you do that your confidence is up for the rest of the season. The rest is easy from there.

You will have bad games during the year for a variety of reasons, but even though I've taken a bit of stick over the years, I've never had any doubt about my own abilities and hopefully I can continue to do a job at Tynecastle.

As Robbo says at the very start of this book, everybody's dream down Gorgie way is finally to take that journey in an open-topped bus through the streets of Edinburgh. We came within one game of that last season, one better this time round would be unforgettable.

I'm lucky enough to have a fair collection of medals and caps, but after so many years of second prizes, holding a trophy with maroon and white ribbons on it would top the lot.

I hope you enjoyed the journey between the two cities as much as I have.